THE *Life* OF
John Birch

*In the story of one American
boy, the ordeal of his age*

by

Robert H. W. Welch, Jr.

HENRY REGNERY COMPANY
Chicago · 1954

For

JOHN T. BROWN

*with admiration
and kindest regards*

FOREWORD

"But on one man's soul it hath broken,
A light that doth not depart;
And his look, or a word he hath spoken
Wrought flame in another man's heart."

UNTIL a little more than a year ago I had never heard of
John Birch. And the links of transmission, through which the
impact of this young man reached me, were thin and strained.
A more tenuous chain of influence could hardly have been
imagined by O'Shaughnessy while writing the above lines of
his great ode.

All alone, in a committee room of the Senate Office Building in Washington, I was reading the dry typewritten pages
in an unpublished report of an almost forgotten congressional
committee hearing. Suddenly I was brought up sharp by a
quotation of some words an army captain had spoken on the
day of his death eight years before. Interest in the quotation
soon led me to the incident with which the following narrative begins. From then on the light of John Birch's actions
gradually became greater than the light of his words, and
neither would depart. With regard to both, I had to learn all
I could of their source and their circumstances. This small
book is the result of my search.

Somewhere in Goethe's thousands of pages appears the
beautiful line: *Alle menschliche Gebrechen sühnet reine
Menschlichkeit.* Pure humanity atones for all human crimes
and weaknesses. As of today this may be too optimistic a
balance sheet. The debit side of the ledger is heavy with mass
murders and inhuman tortures, with blasphemy and treason
and felonies and cruelties, so despicable in degree and so
widespread in practice as to prompt a feeling of despair.

Even the purity of character and nobility of purpose of a John Birch can atone for only a small part of so much human vileness.

But there is strong encouragement in finding so firm an entry on the credit side. For the fact that cultural traditions and ethical forces still at work can produce one such man is clear proof that they are still producing others like him. Of the slowly built hereditary and environmental molds, into which such youth were poured, many have now been smashed altogether, and many more have their sidewalls badly cracked; but many still remain unreached by the stresses of political tyranny and the erosion of moral anarchy around us. The output of these molds can still save our civilization.

It is no accident that you also, who now read these lines, have probably never heard of John Birch before. That small victory of our Communist enemies, in consigning him to temporary oblivion, cannot now be undone. But even with my plodding skill bogging down my bounding purpose, I believe that you will long remember him after finishing these short chapters ahead. And his memory will add, in some small measure, to your hope and your inspiration.

THE LIFE OF JOHN BIRCH

I

The Rescue of Colonel Doolittle

THE TIME is an evening in April, 1942. We have been at war with Japan four and one-half months. Colonel Doolittle's flyers have just startled themselves, the Japanese, and the world with their token bombing of Tokyo. But the planes have no place to land within their fuel range. For China has been at war with Japan *four and one-half years*. The coastal provinces of China are full of occupation troops, which at this very time are beginning new advances inland. The three airfields most counted on have all been bombed, whether through a leak in Washington as suspected by General Stilwell or solely by the accidents of war. At any rate, Doolittle and his fellow pilots simply fly their planes to the Chinese mainland, and over it as long as their gasoline holds out. They then come down with a crash landing, or by parachute.

The place is a cheap restaurant in a village by a river, near the western boundary of Chekiang Province. One of the customers is a young American. He is dressed in cheap native clothes, and speaks the native dialect. He is eating the cheapest native food, by habit as well as by thrifty instinct. For while, at the minute, he has a little more money than usual, he has been living on two dollars per month for the past several months. (Later this ability, gained by hard experience, to subsist on bamboo shoots and the cheapest red rice, is to prove of great value when he becomes the first American ever to live and work *in the field* with a Chinese army. Later, he is to prove his remarkable proficiency at disguising himself and melting

1

away undiscoverably into the native population. But tonight he knows nothing of this future.) Fortunately, while not conspicuous, he is making no attempt to hide his own nationality.

The other patrons of the restaurant are all Chinese. One of them, on his way out after a brief meal, brushes against the stranger as if by accident, and manages to whisper, in Chinese: "If you are an American, please follow me." The stranger, as soon as he dares, also rises and leaves. The incident goes unnoticed by the other diners.

Outside, the American is taken by his self-appointed guide to a small covered riverboat, casually and inconspicuously laid up alongside the river's bank. In that boat he finds Colonel James H. Doolittle, who has been hidden and brought this far by Chinese patriots. This is the first American Doolittle has seen since his raid. The young man is able not only to get Colonel Doolittle safely into free China, but is instrumental in rounding up and saving a number of the men from several of the other planes. Without him it is doubtful that any of these flyers, or their commander himself, would have escaped capture and torture by the Japanese.

I ran across this very small but unusual pebble on the beach of history while looking for some larger and entirely different rocks. It puzzled me, and prompted several questions. (1) Who was this young American? (2) How did he happen to be where he was at this exact and opportune time? (3) What happened to him afterwards? As I dug for the answers they soon led me to more important questions: (4) Why was so heroic, brilliant, and consecrated a patriot so completely unknown in America? And (5) What was the significance of his life—and death? What I found out on all five points is outlined, in part, below. But it is the last two questions that give weight to the whole inquiry. For, as Senator Knowland has stated publicly, if the story of this young man had been known and understood, it could have made a huge difference in our attitude and the circumstances that led to our engagement in Korea.

II

An American Childhood

HIS NAME was John Birch. He was twenty-three years old, and from a farm near Macon, Georgia. A direct descendant of John Alden, John Birch was as American as Calvin Coolidge and "Buffalo Bill" Cody, to both of whom he was related. For although John was proud of the fact that his mother's ancestry had been traced back, clearly and unmistakably, to the time of William the Conqueror, and that three members of that ancestry had been knighted in England, his family on both sides had been deeprooted in America for generations.

It is worth while thus stressing this matter of lineage because of the rather strange coincidence that John Birch, as fine a young man as America has ever produced, was born in Asia and also died in Asia. Perhaps the fact is symbolic of the greater interest America was already taking and must now continue to take in that continent.

His parents, George S. Birch and Ethel Ellis Birch, were—and still are—deeply religious people. For three years of their lives immediately after marriage they were both missionaries in India. Or at least they were so classified by the Mission Headquarters which had sent them to Asia. But Mr. Birch, who had a B.S. Degree in Agriculture from the University of Georgia, actually taught Agriculture at Ewing Christian College in Allahabad, India; ran the college dairy; and then worked with men's Bible classes in all of his spare time. Mrs. Birch, who held a Bachelor of Science Degree from Wooster College, Wooster, Ohio, tutored English at Ewing Christian College and worked with women's Bible classes in as wide

3

an area as she could reach. Their first child, John Morrison Birch, was born on May 28, 1918, in Landaur, India. But when he was two and one-half years old, the family returned to America—primarily because of his father's persistent illness in the Indian climate.

They settled first in his mother's home town, Vineland, New Jersey. George Birch became a partner with his father-in-law in a successful fruit-growing business, Blue Spruce Farms. And there the boy, John Birch, went through grammar school, leading his class. Then, in 1930, Mr. Birch was asked to come back to the Mt. Berry School in Rome, Georgia, where both he and Mrs. Birch had taught before they were married, and where they had first met each other. He accepted, Mrs. Birch and the children—there were now seven—followed a year later, and all but one of John's remaining years in America were spent in Georgia.

For the Birch family of nine the depression decade was a jumble of teaching (on the part of both parents), of farming, of poverty, of the pain of being separated by the available work, of the pleasure of regrouping; of the growing strength of family ties and the sustaining strength of a fundamental faith that made every hardship seem merely a test of character. There was one stretch when the family did not have more than five dollars of actual cash income for three months; there was more than one period of months at a time when they lived almost exclusively on milk toast made from stale "penny" bread. For even when Mr. and Mrs. Birch were both teaching, clothes of some kind had to be bought and other necessities provided for themselves and seven growing children.

Next to the education, religion, and character of his parents, the greatest single influence on John Birch, undoubtedly, was his life at Birchwood, a farm which had belonged to Mr. Birch's father. It consisted of several hundred acres, mostly wooded but part in cultivation, with a large but dilapidated house that had originally been built for the superintendent of a granite quarry, now long since abandoned. This house, a mile up a winding lane from any highway or any neighbor, sat in a beautiful and completely casual growth of trees and vines and shrubs, on a hill that sloped down in a few hundred yards to the steep bank of the Ocmulgee River. Perhaps this writer is prejudiced by similar personal experience, but there is some substance to the feeling that only those who have lived without money on ancestral acres in the South can fully understand the strange mixture of poverty and pride, the attitudes, aspirations, and sense of values generated by such an environment. The hope of some day "fixing up" Birchwood as a worthy home for his parents and the other children remained one of John Birch's freely admitted concessions to human vanity even during all of his years in China, while he was planning a far more ascetic and dedicated career for himself. And when the house at Birchwood burned in September, 1943, without insurance, due to sparks from a railroad locomotive carried to the property by a high wind while the whole family was absent, John's immediate reaction to news of the disaster was to write his parents that—whatever else they did—they should not sell any of their land.

In 1934 Mrs. Birch and the children had been living on a rented farm in Floyd County, Georgia, near where Mr. Birch was teaching Agriculture, and where Mrs. Birch had also been teaching English for the preceding two years. When they decided to go to Birchwood it was a year before Mr. Birch could leave his job and join them. To John, as the oldest child, now sixteen years old, fell most of the responsibility for moving their limited but heterogeneous possessions more than a hundred miles. It was an undertaking, and an adventure, never to be forgotten. He and his brother Ellis went ahead, in a little Model T Ford pick-up truck, to build a small corral in which to keep the cattle temporarily. There were thirty-one head, and when they arrived in a huge trailer truck a few days later, the two resourceful boys had the enclosure finished. After that the cattle had to be put out to graze daily, and "minded" by the younger children, until the older boys could get some fences built. But even every chicken was moved successfully without loss, and every member of the family plunged into the work of making Birchwood really a home. When Mr. Birch did arrive the next summer one "extra" accomplishment they could proudly show him was that they had fenced four hundred acres of the land.

During all these years of moving, of poverty, and of unceasing farm chores, neither John nor any of the children old enough to go to school ever missed a year, or a month. Secular education for their children in the institutions available, religious education in the Sunday Schools and church services nearby, and both secular and religious education continuously at home, constituted together a "must" to which Mr. and Mrs. Birch were willing to sacrifice almost all other considerations —and frequently did. John graduated from Gore High School in Chattooga County, at the head of his class. One year after the family settled at Birchwood John entered Mercer University in Macon, where he led his class, and from which he received his B.A. Degree in 1939, *magna cum laude*. He then went to the Bible Baptist Seminary in Fort Worth, Texas, where he did two years work in one year and still graduated at the head of his class. His impact on that school while he was there, as much as the small part of his fabulous later record which did seep through, is responsible for the fact that one of their buildings was later named John Birch Hall. And his graduation from the Seminary, in June, 1940, brings us up to the second question in our series of five.

III

Early Months in China

JOHN HAD volunteered for missionary work in China while he was still a senior at Mercer. He had already been accepted by the World's Fundamentalist Baptist Missionary Fellowship when he went to Fort Worth. He sailed for China in July, 1940, and never returned.

The first six months, in addition to performing missionary duties of which he was capable, he attended a language school in Shanghai. To a natural genius for languages he added determination and an unceasing desire to continue learning, from every source, after this formal initiation into Chinese. Eventually he acquired a fluency possessed by few Americans. By early in 1941 he could speak the native tongue well enough to be sent to Hangchow, where he taught at a Chinese school for boys, conducted services, and worked with the Chinese ministers in the small churches of a wide area. Here was a preacher, burning with zeal, who really intended to preach. He went out regularly through the Japanese occupation lines to see rural congregations, and visited many villages where no American had been seen since fighting had first reached that area three and one-half years before. He was the only missionary in Hangchow who continued excursions to the country during all the "gathering gloom" (his own phrase) of 1941. And by the time Pearl Harbor came he had so incurred the wrath of the Japanese that on the very first day of official war with America they sent a detachment to arrest John Birch. But he escaped, and fled to Shangjao in Kiangsi Province. There, with funds completely cut off, he and four native preachers sustained and encouraged the little congregations of converts to the best of their abilities—and made more converts. Despite every handicap, one earnest group, blessed by John's guidance and enthusiasm, actually built one small new church during these hectic months.

Not only was John without money, except for the very little he had saved out of his salary of fifty dollars per month, but most of these small savings were in traveler's checks which, after Pearl Harbor, no bank in Kiangsi would cash. Communications with America were impossible. In January there arrived at Shangjao, after a precarious journey from Shanghai through occupied territory, a baptized native who brought a message from missionaries stranded in that city. They asked

7

John to get word to headquarters in Chicago that all funds, any funds, for them, should be sent through John Birch in Shangjao. This was only in part because Shangjao was still in "Free China." It was because John was so inevitably a leader of men, on whom others leaned in times of trouble. Despite his own desperate shortage he relayed this message by radio, cable, and air mail, but no answer came.

One of the native preachers gave up and went to his small home in another province. And by April 15 John was completely destitute. But the turning point was at hand. On April 18, the very day of Doolittle's raid, the Chinese Army Headquarters in Hangchow cashed the traveler's checks which the banks had rejected. John's first thought was of his desperate "brothers" in the North. The native "brother" was still in Shangjao. John gave this man all of the funds he could possibly spare, and set out at once in a small borrowed boat to conduct him down the river into Chekiang Province, to see that he got started as safely as possible on the perilous journey back to Shanghai. Accompanying this emissary as far as Sing Teng, John even visited several of the country churches in that area. Then he returned alone up the river, through the dangerous no-man's land towards Shangjao. It was on this return trip that he stopped to eat in the restaurant where he was accosted by the native who took him to Colonel Doolittle.

IV

The Missionary Becomes a Soldier

BY APRIL, 1942, John Birch was aware that the Japanese would soon overrun Shangjao. He had already written the American Military Mission in Chungking, asking to join the army as a chaplain, as a private, or in whatever capacity he could be most useful. After his encounter with Colonel Doolittle events moved very rapidly, both as to the general developments in that part of China and as to John's own life in the midst of these developments.

At Lanchi he and Colonel Doolittle separated, the Colonel going on to Chungking and John taking the train back to Shangjao. The day he reached that city, April 27, two telegrams arrived. One was money from the Fellowship office in Chicago. The other was from Chungking, ordering him to duty at Ch'u Chou Airbase, and then to go on to the capital city when his work at the airbase was finished. On May 4 he wrote his parents a long letter from Ch'u Chou, concerning his recent activities, and ending with these lines: "This week I have been serving as chaplain to the flyers who bombed Tokyo; now most of them have gone on to Chungking, and when the dead and wounded shall have been cared for, I shall go on, too. Needless to say, please pray. The Japs are bombing here daily now." That last admonition seems to have been well justified. For on the very day that John left Ch'u Chou, four and one-half weeks later, the Japanese bombed the headquarters where he had been living, killing four people.

In the meantime, amazingly and unexpectedly, he had received from his parents a cashable draft for one hundred and ten American "gold" dollars. Nobody knew and appreciated more than John himself how much sacrifice on their part this represented. But it came just in time to help him and the Chinese preachers evacuate before the advancing Japs, who soon captured their mission in Shangjao and overran Ch'u Chou as well.

On May 28, his twenty-fourth birthday, with his chaplain's work in Ch'u Chou finished, John headed for Chungking. Transportation was hard to find, because of the proximity and fierceness of the fighting, the rapidity of the Japanese advance, and the resulting mass evacuation. But with the help of some Chinese officers John finally caught a gasoline truck bound for southern Kiangsi Province. They were held up by floods, washed-out bridges, impassable ferry crossings, and other obstacles, time and time again, but at last reached Heng Yang, in Hunan Province, on June 10. There John got the night train to Kweilin, in Kwangsi Province, where, by a miracle of coincidence, he bumped into General Claire Chennault, Commander of the famous American Volunteer Group. General Chennault gave John a ride in an Army transport plane—his first in any plane—to Chungking, which they reached on June 16. For the next three weeks he served as assistant chaplain to the A.V.G. And on July 4, 1942, he was inducted as a 2nd Lieutenant into the China Air Task Force of the American Army. This unit, which on that very day superseded the simultaneously dissolved American Volunteer Group, remained under the command of General Chennault, and the following March became the 14th Air Force.

Colonel Doolittle, still in Chungking at this time, was very much interested in Chinese aviation. One of John's early but incidental jobs was serving as interpreter for the colonel in conversations with the Chinese flight commanders. This was undoubtedly the hardest language test that John ever faced, for he himself confessed wryly that most of Doolittle's technical terms were not even known to him in English. But he handled the assignment with great satisfaction to everybody concerned, until Colonel Doolittle left China.

It cannot be guessed now whether John Birch, Baptist missionary, would ever have been assigned to Intelligence but for his accidental experience as helper and interpreter for Colonel Doolittle. Certainly John himself had not even thought of this as a possibility, as his letters clearly reveal. But hindsight makes it evident that few men have been better equipped for the work by training, or better suited to it by character. He had many assets for the purpose in addition to those which have already been mentioned.

One of the most important and useful of these assets was his elementary but adequate knowledge of radio, plus a natural mechanical aptitude. At Birchwood, when John was sixteen years old and the family was too poor to buy a radio, he and Ellis had built their own. Now, during the next three years, he was to become a technical expert, at installing, repairing, and operating radio equipment, in all kinds of places and under the most adverse conditions.

For about eight months John worked directly under and very close to General Chennault, as an Intelligence Officer, in Chungking and then in Kunming. Not too much is known of his activities during this period, but some light is thrown on them by a letter written by Chennault in November, 1942. Dated at Kunming, on stationery of Headquarters, China Air Task Force, it is addressed to 2nd Lt. John M. Birch, 23d Fighter Group, and reads as follows:

> 1. Your recent secret mission in relation to intelligence matters, which led you extremely close to enemy territory, has been invaluable to the China Air Task Force. The successful accomplishment of this hazardous mission required fortitude, courage, and devotion to duty. The excellent manner in which you have carried out this difficult duty is highly commended.
> 2. A copy of this letter will be placed in your 201 file.
> C. L. Chennault
> Brigadier General, A.U.S. Commanding

It is also known that, without previous training, John arranged the organization and correction of maps, records, and incoming information, and practically established the Intelligence Headquarters of the newly created China Air Task Force.

Then, in March, 1943, when this group became the 14th Air Force, and was augmented in strength by the 308th Bomb Group, John was sent to Changsha, as Liaison and Intelligence Officer with Marshal Hsueh Yo, Commander of the Chinese Ninth War Area. He soon won the complete confidence and lasting respect of this general; and with extremely limited facilities was able to set up a steady flow of intelligence information back to headquarters. The result was that, for the first time, air support of the Chinese troops by the 14th Air Force was made possible by knowledge of where these troops were and what they were trying to do. But all of John's excellent achievements in this more routine work were completely overshadowed by his exploits in the field. There are many reports, some couched in much more official language, concerning these activities of John Birch, from both American and Chinese sources—and there are probably some in the Japanese archives, too, if they could be uncovered. But perhaps the best is a very short and informal statement by Colonel Wilfred Smith, which reads in part as follows:

"—About the time of John's arrival in Changsha, the Japanese were preparing another offensive. John gave us early warning of enemy intentions and made it possible for us to bomb supply columns as they were forming, as well as supply dumps. As soon as the offensive gained momentum John, with a portable radio set, accompanied Chinese troops to the front line and observed the hour-to-hour shifts in the enemy attack. During the whole campaign John kept the 14th Air Force headquarters advised by radio of the enemy attack. He had not had any formal training in the operation of a radio but soon learned to master the technique and was on the air constantly talking to pilots as they attacked. He would say 'White Pontiac, do you see my white panels?' John would have huge strips of cloth on the ground with arrow pointing to the target. The pilot would say 'Roger, boy, Roger.' Then John would say, 'There is a howitzer over there about a quarter of a mile just northeast of that pagoda.' The answer would come back 'Roger.' Then John would say, 'Hold it, you are shooting over,' and then he would say, 'Bring it down, that's it, you got it that time.'

"We called that kind of work 'air-ground liaison.' John would be in sight of these targets he was calling. The pilots used to talk about how much help it was, and often said it was like being led by the hand to the target. John spent about six weeks with the Chinese troops in the 1943 Tungting Lake campaign, and we called him the eyes of the 14th Air Force. This is the first time, to my knowledge, that Chinese troops ever knew what efficient air support could do, and the experience certainly heightened the morale of the Chinese troops immeasurably. General Hsueh said that if he had fifty teams like the one John handled he could lick the Japs himself singlehanded. But we

12

just didn't have radios and men. If John should break a tube it would be all my life was worth just to get one tube."

There were many incidental or additional benefits to the American-Chinese allies, from this one-man intelligence offensive, which are not covered in these paragraphs from Colonel Smith's report. For one thing it was, as General Chennault had said, the first time any American—even a war correspondent—had ever been able to stay *in the field* with a Chinese Army, and live. John Birch proved to his fellow Americans that it could be done, and many other brave and hardy souls—mostly ex-missionaries—followed his example and carried out similar tasks. But what was equally important, was proving this fact to the Chinese. They thought that Americans were so accustomed to living in the lap of luxury—which they were by Chinese standards—that they could not really be very good ground soldiers. John Birch proved that he could get along on exactly the same rations, and live continuously under the same conditions, that they did, and still fight and work twenty hours a day. By his own stamina and character John so improved relations of the Americans with the Chinese in the Ninth War Area that he was able to arrange an effective rescue system for American pilots shot down behind the Japanese lines. Colonel Smith says further along: "John set that up himself. I would conservatively estimate that about fifty American pilots were saved by the system which John organized in 1943-44." And General Chennault said, in 1945, that about ninety per cent of his downed flyers had been saved by John's rescue arrangements—the highest percentage in any war theatre.

In the long official commendation of John Birch by Major General Charles B. Stone, one other significant result of these field activities is recorded. "Early in 1944, in the Hunan combat area, he organized and conducted a school for Chinese Army radio operators and cryptographers for ground-air coordination parties, training well over a hundred of these critically needed individuals." Further along General Stone adds:

13

"During all of these phases he sent back to Fourteenth Air Force Headquarters by radio a constant stream of invaluable combat and political intelligence."

And the final word on John's services in Hunan can appropriately be given to General Hsueh Yo himself. On December 14, 1943, he sent an official communication to "Major General C. L. Chennault, C.C., 14th U.S. Air Force" on the subject "Tribute paid to 1st Lieutenant John M. Birch." It read, in translation, as follows:

"During the whole of this Changteh campaign, the diligent and efficient service of 1st Lt. John M. Birch, liaison and intelligence officer of the 14th U.S. Air Force on detached service in this war zone, who has worked continuously day and night without taking rest, contributed greatly to the close cooperation of the ground and air troops and to the happy conclusion of the said campaign. It is requested that he be given high merits for his brilliant service."

> General Hsueh Yo
> Commanding General
> Ninth War Zone

This message was forwarded to John by General Chennault, with an extremely commendatory message of his own. It ended: "Your successes will play an important part in finally driving the Japanese from China."

They did.

V

An Expedition to the Yangtze

YEARS LATER Chennault, in his autobiographical history, *The Way Of A Fighter,* was to write: "John Birch was the pioneer of our field-intelligence net." Applications of

14

the word "pioneer" to John Birch recur so frequently in comments concerning his career, from all sources, that we shall be unable ourselves to avoid repeating the term without omitting material and quotations needed for other purposes. To be the pioneer, and chart both purpose and course, under the prevailing circumstances, however, required endowments of a superior order. A physical and mental imperviousness to privation and hardship, even for long periods of time, was one of John's assets for intelligence work that we have already glanced at in passing. It deserves a longer look.

Since it is not the custom of Intelligence men to do much talking about their exploits, and since John Birch was, according to all reports, about the least loquacious of this reticent lot, there are many of his trips, and many months of his life, about which we have almost no information. We know, for instance, that at some time and for some purpose he made the difficult journey to Tibet—nothing more. We know that he once rode a Mongolian pony sixty miles through a snowstorm over rough terrain, in one day—but not when or why. Nevertheless the known facts were sufficient to make his hardihood a legend.

Part of this ability came from mental attitude and determination. But part of it came from a splendid youthful physique, with tremendous recuperative powers, and with a camel-like ability to refuel for long stretches whenever the opportunity offered. During John's months in Chungking, after his arrival there in June, 1942, his appetite had been regarded with amazement by everybody. Headquarters of Chennault's A.V.G., and of the Task Force which succeeded it, were at Peishiyi Air Base, actually some thirty miles out of Chungking, and the food provided this group by the Chinese at this time was excellent and plentiful. But John would eat a large dinner, which filled everybody else up, and then turn right around and eat a second dinner, just like the first, starting with soup and straight on through dessert. His system was recovering strength and substance after those long months on bamboo shoots and rice; and was automatically, if without conscious intention, preparing for even more months ahead when it would have to get along exclusively on similar sustenance again.

In August, 1943, during a lull between the two Changteh campaigns, John left Changsha with two Chinese radio operators and six coolies. All he took with him was one case of D rations, a tommy gun, and a .45 pistol; and some scant bedding and several radios which were carried by the coolies. His mission was to contact General Shuen Yoh who commanded, in the Hankow-Wuning-Wienning triangle, a hard-hitting guerilla outfit known euphemistically as the 2nd Group Brigade. In between were mountains, areas of scorching semi-tropical heat, and the enemy. The only beverage to be drunk with safety was boiled water, or tea; and about the only food available behind the lines was "red rice with rocks in it." John himself had sufficient respect for the danger involved to have left in Changsha this message: "If anything should happen to me please tell my family I am deeply grateful for my Christian home and upbringing." But he and his little troupe walked the three hundred miles, averaging thirty miles per day—and back again. Although he had completely worn out two pairs of Army shoes, and actually reached Changsha in Chinese cloth sandals, John returned safely in October, "lean, deeply sunburned, but in splendid condition, and greatly inspired with the success of his mission."

He had found the Chinese guerillas completely cooperative and helpful. "While on the Yangtze," General Chennault reports, "Birch discovered the Japanese were much more dependent on the Shihweiyao iron mines and smelter than we had suspected. He sent us detailed information that enabled us to cripple the blast furnaces and docks by bombing."

On this same mission John learned through his guerilla friends that the Japanese were using a suburb near Hankow to conceal a big munitions dump from air attacks on that city. After this information was transmitted by radio relays to headquarters the bombers were still unable to locate the target. So John himself filtered back through the lines far enough to

16

be picked up by a plane, and rode in the nose of the lead B-25 to pin-point the exact spot for the bombardier. When the first bombs hit, munitions started exploding, and soon the whole seemingly deserted town erupted into a volcano of smoke and fire. John's Chinese friends, who had tipped him off to this secret, were watching from a nearby hill, and were greatly impressed by what he had been able to accomplish. When he later made his way forward to that area once more, to continue his expedition, they told him that the dump had been completely destroyed.

Most important result of the whole mission, however, was John's establishment of tiny radio stations overlooking the main river ports, including one such station on a small island right in the Yangtze. "From this station," 1st Lt. Arthur H. Hopkins, Jr., who was carrying on John's radio mission in Changsha while he was gone, has written, "the Chinese radio operators sent into the 14th Air Force reports of Japanese shipping along the most important waterways, and daily weather reports." This station and others John set up "worked back to him" in Changsha; from where he translated and relayed the information to 14th Air Force Headquarters. And as Colonel Wilfred Smith put it, through John's placing those sets on the river, from then on "the Japs never moved a ship on the Yangtze without our knowledge."

Hopkins wrote further: "John was a pioneer in this type of work, and completed many missions of this nature. Some of the time he disguised himself as a Chinese coolie, even carrying a load from a bamboo pole across his shoulders. He spoke Chinese so perfectly that the natives all thought he was a Chinese from another province." Very few Americans could get away with this, and, as we have already remarked, it was a tremendously valuable accomplishment to have such a command of the language; but probably even fewer Americans could survive the work and the living conditions, required to be convincing as a Chinese coolie, for any worthwhile length of time.

In October John Birch and Arthur Hopkins together set up

17

a new and much larger radio station in Changsha, John having gone to Kunming for the personnel and equipment immediately on his return from the Yangtze expedition. Hopkins was transferred early in November, and John personally handled most of the liaison work during the battle for Changteh in November and December. Once again, while this battle lasted, he worked twenty hours a day for a stretch of several weeks.

In February, 1944, John went to Kunming again for more supplies. He spent the month of March further improving the operation in Changsha, and then the station was taken over by Captain Malcolm Rosholt. For the 14th Air Force was now ready to start extending its operations further north. And John Birch, because of both his skill and enthusiasm as a trail blazer, was sent to pioneer the intelligence and liaison work north of the Yangtze Kiang. His usefulness, and the importance of his work, were to increase greatly in this new theatre of the war.

VI

Settling Down in Anhwei

Now SOLID experience, and the complete confidence of his superiors and fellow officers, helped to make more valuable one asset which he had possessed from the beginning. That was an extremely practical approach to the total job to be done. For John Birch intelligence and liaison work was never a matter of going through certain motions or prescribed procedures, or a thing apart for him to do as his particular duty and for somebody else to make effective. The idea was to drive the Japs out of China. John saw anything and everything that might contribute to that end as a part of his own job.

Major General Stone, in his official commendation of John Birch for the Distinguished Service Cross, from which we have already quoted, summarized a part of John's activities for about twelve months in one paragraph as follows:

"Having participated until mid-1944 in the early stages of the final North-South Japanese drive, and having organized a highly successful supply-dropping operation for the hard-pressed Chinese ground troops, he was designated to go on a political mission into the Japanese-held northern province of Shantung. But on his way there a strategic situation having developed in the intermediate province of Anhwei, and receiving orders to assist the Chinese Army Commander there, he spent several months until spring, 1945, developing intelligence in the area and, during the course of his stay, organized the construction of two secret airfields adjacent to Japanese-held territory, from which a number of forced-down air personnel were rescued, and successfully took off again, key supplies for forward Chinese units and important undercover agents were landed at a saving of many weeks of otherwise unavoidable ground travel. These fields were used on several occasions as refueling points on extended combat missions."

This paragraph, accurate and completely appropriate for its purpose, is nevertheless suggestive of the condensation, by the Persian scholars in Anatole France's story, of the history of the whole human race into "They were born, they suffered, they died." Since ours is not an official report, we can afford to look at a little of the detail behind this condensation.

Actually, the mission to the north was decided on at a conference in Kunming between Colonel Jesse Williams and Colonel Wilfred Smith in which John participated. The idea was to have John do in North China what he had already done so successfully in South China; establish widespread and useful liaison and intelligence in the field. The fact that almost everything north of the Yangtze was enemy-held territory, and that there were at this time three million Japanese in China, approximately one-half of them in the armed forces, does not seem to have discouraged either John or his superiors in the least.

The operation was planned to begin with three men; 1st Lt. (later Captain) William Drummond, Sergeant Eichenberry (a good radio man), and John—now Captain—Birch. Captain Birch was to be in charge, and Colonel Williams issued the final order on March 17. Drummond and Eichenberry went ahead with supplies, John went back to Changsha to wind things up there, and they met at Lao Ho Kow on May 17, 1944.

At that time the Japs were starting their campaign along the Pinghan Railway, having already taken Loyang and occupied the old right of way with their troops. Perhaps this had something to do with the orders John received to stop in Anhwei instead of going on to Shantung Province. At any rate he and Drummond and Eichenberry stayed at Lao Ho Kow until May 26, and then took off with one Chinese officer in the direction of Fowyang. Proceeding by foot they arrived on June 6th at the small town of Shenchiu, and decided that this was it. They set up their radio station in Shenchiu.

From June 6 through September 6 one of the party was always at Shenchiu, and this was their central point of contact. During the first part of this period, or about June 15, the first B-29 raid on Japan occurred. The planes flew right over Shenchiu that night and then early in the morning flew back over Shenchiu in the opposite direction. Their fate was unknown to John or his crew for some time. But the flight had been a great help, nevertheless. For the Chinese in that area had not been able to see how the Americans and their radio station could possibly do any good there. This visible evidence of the reach of American airpower changed their minds and made the mission considerably easier.

In the meantime, immediately on arrival and entirely on his own initiative, John had started looking for possible locations for emergency airfields. He found two promising spots, the nearest one about fifty miles away. With Chinese officers and the aid of Chinese engineers, all of whom he had to persuade that the project was worth while, he went out himself and laid out the rough dimensions and plans for the field. (One summer back in Georgia, between college years, John had worked on a surveying crew. The experience probably helped a little now, simply in giving him a better understanding of the task.) Then the Chinese did the job of actual construction, entirely by hand labor, and the whole field did not cost the U. S. Air Force a penny. The same was true of the second field built. John was able to get almost incredible cooperation and enthusiastic support from both the Chinese armed forces and Chinese civilians, because he knew how to deal with them diplomatically in their own language and because his sincere friendship for the Chinese and devotion to their cause were so unmistakable. For a few weeks there were literally thousands of coolies working on this field, building the strips by the most primitive labor methods known.

Then a very ill wind for one of his crew was converted by John into a very good wind for his general purpose. Sergeant Eichenberry came down sick, very sick. The Chinese physician identified the disease as cholera. John got a radio message through to Kunming recommending that they send a plane out there to evacuate Eichenberry. It was always hard to get the Air Force to use a temporary field. So John's idea was not only to get Eichenberry out, but also to force the issue by getting a plane in and thus breaking the ice for the use of his new field. And so, on July 19, only six weeks after John Birch had first reached Shenchiu, the Chinese American Composite Wing sent a B-25 bomber and eight P-40's as an escort to this field which his Chinese friends had built. They picked up Eichenberry and took him out. They dropped a few supplies, the first John's mission had had, except what they brought with them. And the new field was in business; established as a forward base which saved about half the distance for normal operations and enabled the 14th Air Force to extend their striking range several hundred miles.

Birch and Drummond went back then to Shenchiu and worked together there for about four weeks. Then on August 13 John got himself picked up at one of his "temporary" fields and taken back to Kunming. But he had arranged that the same plane which took him out brought in Sergeant Lee, an American-born Chinese radio operator, so that Drummond and Lee could maintain effective radio headquarters at Shenchiu while he was gone.

The purpose of John's trip was to report to headquarters, to discuss the prospects of using his Shenchiu mission and the two airfields for forward air bases and as a central source of intelligence for North China and Manchuria—and to obtain supplies and equipment. He was successful in all particulars, even and especially in convincing headquarters of the value of the enterprise. He arrived back at one of the airfields on October 18, in a transport, accompanied by a C-47 loaded with freight. Altogether he brought back between five and six thousand pounds of radio equipment and supplies. He also brought back Lt. Lu, one of his old radio operators from the Changsha station. The two Americans, Captain Birch and Lt. Drummond, and the two Chinese, Lt. Lu and Sergeant Lee, then worked together at Shenchiu until November 2. They were justifiably proud of the fact that, at the end of the longest supply line in the world, which was the China theatre, they were at the end of the longest branch in that area—850 miles by air from Kunming—and were functioning so well.

As soon as they had all of the additional equipment properly nailed down, both Birch and Drummond agreed they should split off and reach out for new contacts. They both left Shenchiu on November 2. But before Drummond got too far word reached him that postponed these excursions. It might be well to quote Lt. Drummond's own report here for a while.

"We got information that flyers from the B-20 raid back in June had been downed near Nanking and that they were being directed out of the Communist area. I headed off toward the temporary airfield, and the [first] flyers pulled in there on November 4. I contacted John and asked him to come down to this airfield so we could get the plane to evacuate these men, which he did. John came down by bicycle and horseback . . .

bringing with him radio supplies. We finally made arrangements to have a transport flown in to pick up these men. Incidentally, they were pretty glad to see us, as we were the first Americans they had seen since they were forced down.

"A curious thing occurred the day the plane was to be flown in, November 15. It started to rain early in the morning, so we sent the word in, figuring that there was no chance the plane would come in that day. At noon that day the Chinese planned a special feast for us. We were eating goat meat. Although it was raining, we were supposed to go out to make contact every hour until ordered by headquarters to secure, but it was raining so hard we figured no plane would come. But John said since it was near the hour, and no orders had come, he would go out anyway to see. So he went out there and he hadn't been gone more than three quarters of an hour when we heard engine noise. Well, everybody broke for the door and the airfield, through the knee-deep mud. I took off on foot, but never made it at all. These 20th Air Force boys [the downed flyers] went on Chinese ponies and outdistanced me. None of the flyers knew how to ride and one riderless pony came by, and the riders went staggering on in the mud. But all got to the plane, though they left their stuff behind.

"There was no escort [for the transport plane] and it surely was bad weather. John was up at the other end of the field with the radio. The field itself was 3,500 feet long. I got down there and John was standing watching the plane take off. He was absolutely dazed and it was five minutes before I could get the story out of him. What had happened was, he had gone out to the field, taking with him a portable direction finder; and while he was tuning in the radio he thought he heard engine noise, but couldn't see anything, the rain was driving so hard. Incidentally, the wind had blown the roof off the temporary radio hut out there, and the rain was coming down on the radio equipment. It was lucky he had brought the finder along (engine noise under rain conditions doesn't give accurate direction), and got a fix on the plane and gave the pilot enough instructions to be able to make a landing. Without these instructions the pilot could not have found the strip and would have had to return without landing.

"When I got there John was standing, soaked to the skin, holding a carton of cigarettes in one hand and the portable direction finder in the other. He said to me 'You can have these. I don't smoke and the pilot says this is his last trip in China, he won't need them.'

"Ordinarily the operation of landing a plane in this field under these circumstances would require at least three men; one to operate the hand-driven generator, one to operate the large transmitter and receiver, and the third to stand outside the hut to give directions to those inside, and to talk the plane in. Actually what John did was to operate the transmitter and generator on the large radio in the rain until the plane was within range of the portable direction finder, and then talk the plane in with this portable outfit. While the plane was landing he had to run on foot to a spot on the field near enough to the plane so the pilot could see him as he served as transient guide, so the plane could taxi to an appropriate spot for unloading and loading. He then had to run ahead of the take-off as the pilot knew nothing of the field.

"It is always dangerous business to bring a plane in, in a temporary field, because radio silence has to be broken and any Jap planes in the area could locate the field and might destroy the plane. Also the plane had to carry enough fuel for the return trip (fuel was as valuable as blood at that time and it took more than eight hundred gallons just for one way), and the plane could waste no time on the ground. With the rain and every condition against him, the split-minute efficiency left John unnerved. He could hardly believe the plane had come and gone when it was all over."

It's no wonder that another one of John Birch's associates in the war, in sending his wife a photograph of John, inscribed on it: "Keep this picture; I can tell you endless stories of him!" And perhaps the quality or asset of John Birch which we should have stressed most was dependability; an unceasing attention to duty at whatever infinite pains might be required. For a failure to contact that rescue plane and bring it in and get it off with every flyer—however excusable and understandable such a failure could have been under the circumstances— might have given John's whole Shenchiu operation a black eye, and caused a loss of absolute confidence back at head-

quarters, which would have greatly reduced the importance
and effectiveness of the mission and of John's further enter-
prising efforts in the future.

VII

A Christmas Party

JOHN BIRCH had many characteristics which might
not have been assets, for an intelligence-liaison job, in everybody, but which certainly were for him. For one thing, he
neither drank, nor smoked, nor swore. But he avoided all the
possible bad effects of this almost fanatical personal asceti-
cism by a complete tolerance of the habits of others, by a constant deprecation of any possible claims to virtue on his part,
and by a rollicking humor. His favorite remark, by radio or
in person, to anybody who was not coming through promptly
enough or fully enough with the cooperation he thought
called for, was: "What's the matter, don't you want to win
this war?" John himself was an unswervingly fundamentalist
Baptist. But he once wrote his parents of his delight on the
arrival at his station of an officer who was an ardent Christian
of another denomination—and then added slyly: "Of course, I
do hope he gets a good immersion sometime soon." And one
of his perennial jokes was about the way the Chinese managed
to grow so many rocks in their rice.

Perhaps humor is not the word to describe the trait in John
Birch about which we are talking, but human-ness. He once
told Arthur Hopkins that he considered PX supplies a "frivo-
lous luxury which saps the morale of an army." And yet he
was notorious for buying PX supplies for enlisted men under
him, on the basis of loans whenever they were short of money,

and then never allowing the loans to be repaid. John fully appreciated the dramatic incongruities which were a frequent part of the incidents of war. As when 1st Lt. T. J. Gribbs parachuted to earth, in what he thought was an extremely rural and remote part of China—which it was—and almost immediately found himself in the midst of a large party, of Americans and Chinese, singing Christmas carols and enjoying the usual Christmas festivities (even including a Santa Claus, who was a Chinese dressed for the part)—with an active radio station at hand to take care of such emergencies as his own.

This was at Linchuan, a small town near Shenchiu, in December, 1944. At the airfield some fifty miles away, living under the most crowded conditions imaginable, and even then only through the limitless hospitality of the self-sacrificing Chinese neighbors, were a large number of both destitute missionaries and "lost" flyers, waiting to be evacuated. But snow had made the field unusable, and finally had got so deep that the field couldn't even be found or recognized under the fourteen-inch blanket. At the time, Lt. Drummond was there with these charges, while John was working at Linchuan. The Chinese commander for this whole area, General Wang, had taken a great liking to John, understood what John and the mission were trying to accomplish, and did everything he possibly could to be helpful. The Christmas party was arranged by General Wang. John sent a message to the field. Lt. Drummond explained to the missionaries, most of whom were quite elderly, that absolutely nothing could be done for a few days anyway, and he and the flyers made Linchuan in two and one-half days on horseback. The Chinese exerted every effort to see that all of the Americans had a good time, and the whole interlude was a wonderful break.

In the meantime Tom Gribbs, of the 32nd Fighter Squadron of the 14th Air Force, had been compelled by a leak in his gas line to drop out of a formation in which he was flying a P-40. Not knowing where he was, he had picked out a spot about ten miles from Linchuan and come down to attempt a landing. Finding that he couldn't make it, he had taken his

26

plane back up and bailed out. He was picked up by Chinese guerillas and taken into Linchuan—to find this Christmas party in full swing. He probably hasn't fully recovered from his amazement yet.

The pilotless plane nose-dived to earth not too far away. One week later a long line of coolies pulled up to the house at which John and Lt. Drummond were staying in Linchuan. John went out to ask them what they were doing, and they said, "Here's your plane." And with a tremendous crash they dropped it in the courtyard. One hundred and twenty of them had lifted the tangled wreck out of the earth and bodily carried it across country to Linchuan.

As badly mangled as it was, John and his associates thought that, under these circumstances, they certainly ought to salvage something from the remains. So he and Drummond and Gribbs rummaged through it thoroughly; but the best they could come up with was the rubber-tired tail wheel, which they used as the foundation for a new wheelbarrow. Or so they thought, but General Wang had a better idea. He got the Americans to melt down the aluminum fuselage, and out of it he had his metal smith make two bathtubs, which he presented to John and Lt. Drummond. If they could only have stayed at Linchuan long enough they could have been living in luxury.

There was one other result of this plane crash which was much more amusing to John. In all of the efforts of Drummond and himself, they were passively opposed by an old-style Chinese general in the area, who never could understand what they were doing, and who had no faith in any modern gadgets or scientific improvements. This General Chow was friendly enough, but just unconvinced. He made a visit to the house where John and Drummond were staying to see how they were getting along. John took him out back to see Gribb's plane. General Chow looked at this tangled mass of scrap, scratched his head, and said: "This airplane business, it still hasn't been perfected." Then he wanted to know how badly the pilot was hurt in landing it. Suddenly it dawned on John

27

that not only had the general probably never heard of a parachute, but that obviously he thought this was the normal result of landing any plane whenever one came down. So John, without enlightening him, solemnly explained that the pilot, who knew his "airplane business" quite well, had not been hurt at all; and then took great delight in introducing the evidently unharmed Gribbs to the astounded general. Months later John Birch was still chuckling over, and enjoying telling friends about, General Chow's obvious mystification.

The missionaries at the airfield were themselves just one episode of a war-long story. From the beginning John had felt a personal responsibility for helping the stranded missionaries, of all denominations. Colonel Wilfred Smith has written, of the earlier—South China—period: "No one will ever know exactly how many missionaries were aided in their evacuation by John. . . . He would stick his neck out. When he was with me he would get an airplane and evacuate them. But John always sent back [with the missionaries] an important packet of military information, which justified his asking for the plane."

This particular lot at the airfield in December, 1944, were China Inland Mission people who had been stranded in the Tenth War Area. They had received orders to leave and report to Chungking, but couldn't get back. John had been in touch with some of them on his own initiative, and had got the word spread around as to where they were to rendezvous. At the time, Lt. Drummond, who had started earlier for Chinese Tenth War Area headquarters at Lihuang, had been obliged to go back to the airbase with more American flyers he had gathered up and others who were coming in. It was an unusually cold winter, rivers were frozen, there was a lot of snow, traveling was miserable, the field was useless, and there was no place at first for even Drummond and the flyers to live except in the tiny quarters at the field. Then about December 20 these missionaries—American, British, and Dutch women, almost all of them over sixty—began to arrive. John had already made arrangements with the Air Force to include

28

these people on the next plane that came in to evacuate flyers. (Lt. Drummond says: "I don't think the missionaries ever realized what a favor this was that John took upon himself— it was difficult to accomplish.") But Drummond, who had himself barely got back to the field with flyers who had been brought to him by guerillas at Kushi, knew nothing of these arrangements. The missionaries enlightened him. They wanted to know if he was Lieutenant Drummond, and if this was the place to which they had been directed for evacuation by instructions of Captain Birch. Drummond decided that undoubtedly the answer to both questions was yes, but what to do with these women had him stumped. His report to John on the radio was a masterpiece. "Harvey's Restaurant," he said, "is absolutely jammed. I hope you are not sending any more customers." The day was saved by a Chinese family, with a fairly large house, moving out of whole sections of it and turning these parts over to Drummond's refugees. Even then food and fuel was a tough problem.

On January 4 Drummond and the flyers left Linchuan and returned to the airfield—arriving in the midst of another snowstorm. When the snow stopped and the weather cleared, it turned even colder, and he and John were becoming pretty desperate to get their charges out. So, at the rather terrible risk of Japanese attack, from exposing the bare black strip of the airfield in such a wide expanse of white, they made the field usable by the most fundamental expedient. All it required was incredible cooperation from the native inhabitants of the area, such as only men like William Drummond and John Birch could obtain. Working against the danger of a thaw, which would make their work a waste and the field useless for another month, between 750 and 800 Chinese went out with hand shovels, day after day in the bitter cold, and simply carried the snow off the field. John got a plane in, early on the morning of January 14. All of the flyers, and all of the missionaries but one, a man, were able to get aboard. He got out on the next plane, one month later.

29

VIII

The O.S.S. Comes to China

BILL DRUMMOND described John Birch as "absolutely fearless, completely unselfish, never thinking of his personal discomfort or danger." This expresses the amazingly unanimous appraisal of everybody who knew him in China. But it is not to be supposed, from this consecrated attitude toward his work, that John was by any means an automaton; or that he was devoid of normal human ambitions and emotions, simply because he kept them so firmly in check.

For one thing, there was a stubbornness about John Birch, when he felt sure he was right, that was a tough obstacle for anybody who needed to break it down. This streak showed up most emphatically, in the form of his personal loyalty to General Chennault, when the Office of Strategic Services began taking over intelligence and liaison work in China late in 1944. John thought the change was both unfair and unwise. He wasn't having any. And he stated publicly, and officially, that he had rather work as a private for Chennault than as a colonel for the O.S.S.

This was not in the least because he put his personal preferences over a sense of duty. For during all these hard thirty months, or more, what John had wanted most was to become a fighter pilot. Somehow, in the midst of everything else, he had learned to fly, had flown some of the small training ships the Chinese had available, and had passed the physical requirements to enter an Army flying school back in the States. As Arthur Hopkins puts it, "he did not feel that he was doing enough, walking around behind enemy lines, but wanted to be in there shooting." He had been promised the opportunity, and pleaded more than once to have it fulfilled. But the opportunity never materialized, simply because John was too valuable as a liaison officer. By his work in the field he made himself, in the eyes of Chennault and many others, "more valuable than a dozen pilots." Edwin James used to say frequently, on pointing John out to his fellow officers, "There goes the most important *one* man in our China operations." Exaggerated though this may have been, the appraisal of Captain Birch's superiors was too nearly the same for him to be spared. So John was denied his request each time, and went on making himself still more valuable as an intelligence and liaison officer.

But John, and others like him, starting from scratch in a country overrun by the enemy, had built up an intelligence and liaison service that was practical, efficient, sparked by unshakable confidence of its members in each other, and increasingly successful. To have men from the European front, who knew nothing of China or the Chinese people, coming in and taking over, through the simple leverage of having all the money allotted to them by Washington, was a bitter pill for a lot of people besides John Birch. Also, John was entirely too intelligent, and by this time too experienced, not to recognize some of the undercurrents that were already starting to cut the ground out from under our Chinese allies, with whom he and the rest of Chennault's forces had been working in marvelously close unison for years.

The result was that his superiors let the matter ride for quite a while, and John was carried for some months as a member of the 14th Air Force after the rest of the intelligence crew had been assigned to O.S.S. But regardless of the wisdom of the course, or the reasons behind it, the O.S.S. did take over. General Chennault has said, "In the spring of 1945 I was ordered to transfer my Intelligence Service—my entire Intelligence organization—to O.S.S. In order to continue to get intelligence, I had to leave my men in the O.S.S., but they still gave me intelligence reports and still rescued my men." John's anomalous position finally became too embarrassing to maintain. Colonel Wilfred Smith argued with him at great length, and General Chennault himself radioed John to come to Kunming for a talk. Chennault pointed out how dependent he and the 14th Air Force still were on their former intelligence team, even though the members of that team had to work now for the O.S.S. It was arranged that Captain Birch would serve as officially "on loan" to the O.S.S., rather than being formally transferred. And it was on this "detached service" basis that John operated under O.S.S. orders, from May, 1945 for the remainder of the war—and of his life. The fact that he received no further promotions in rank may have been due to his peculiar status. For the newcomers to China in the O.S.S. came rapidly to share the universal admiration for him as a man and as an officer, and a continued dependence on him for the most difficult missions.

John had clearly foreseen the basic significance of some of the moves taking place, including the intention to brush Chennault aside; and had contributed his own one-man fight against it as a matter of principle in which he deeply believed. But during these very months when the protracted argument was going on, he had been doing his most important work of the war to date. In February he had gone to headquarters in Kunming for further plans and orders. Thereafter, he was all over China for a while, on various coordination tasks. In March he was back in Linchuan once more, to help establish an actual base there. Then, with a permanent team of about ten men, and more men drawn from the 10th Chinese Air Force as needed, he was constantly establishing new bases, and bringing in personnel to man them. Again referring to Major General Stone's official summary, we find that "in April, 1945, he [John] supervised the placement of ten American air-ground coordination units out of Sian in North China which, operating with the Chinese Army in conjunction with 14th Air Force units, were largely instrumental in containing the Japanese drive from Honan Province towards Sian."

It was apparently at the end of these particular efforts that John caught plane rides a thousand miles to Kunming—the official version is that he "hitchhiked"—for his conversation with General Chennault that led to his "temporary" attachment to O.S.S. in May. His continuous job, from then on until the end of the war in August, was the organizing of undercover intelligence activities in North China.

In the three years from May, 1942, when John Birch headed across Kiangsi Province for Chungking, expecting to be a chaplain, to May, 1945, when he joined O.S.S., John had matured a great deal. He himself, in a letter written during March, 1944, expressing his humble regret that he had not been living up to his high evangelical Christian purpose with all the unremitting zeal of which he felt he should have been capable, found one consoling thought for himself and for the equally devout aunt to whom he poured out his faith and his meditations. (This aunt, Miss May Cosman, a much loved teacher in the public schools of Landis Township, New Jersey, had first taught John to read when he was four years old, while the family was living in Vineland. Really his great-aunt—his mother's aunt—, she had contributed to his support while in college, helped him in many other ways, and exerted a strong influence over his whole life. John was a very loyal and grateful nephew.) "Meantime," he wrote, as though in self defense, "I am growing (in the arm of flesh) in ability to organize and handle men in the achievement of difficult tasks. So these years of violence are not entirely wasted." He then added a strikingly prophetic line: *"I believe that this war and the ensuing federations will set the world stage, as never before, for the rise of anti-Christ!"* And he closed by declaring what a privilege it would be, in that day, to fight on the Christian side.

Unfortunately, agents of the very anti-Christ, whose rise John foresaw, also recognized what a dangerous antagonist John Birch would be. For it was his firm intention, often announced, to remain in China and resume his missionary activities once the war was over. He had even given as one reason for learning to fly that with a small plane he would be able to multiply many fold his efforts in organizing new missions and

33

churches and in keeping them strong and growing. His consecration to this dream was so great and so positive that for it he made, of his own free will, what must have been an extremely heavy sacrifice.

IX

The One Romance

SOMEHOW, DURING these three years, John Birch had also found time to fall in love and become engaged. Contrary to what might be surmised from the puritan rigor of his existence and his assured self-discipline, John had an intensely romantic outlook on everything about life, including love. On successfully reaching the Yangtze Kiang at the end of his three hundred mile expedition through enemy territory in 1943, John had been so excited and pleased that he had reached down and scooped up some of the water with his hands and drunk it (even though he well knew the danger and did not usually take any needless risk of his life or his health). And he himself had said that he felt very much like Balboa discovering the Pacific. This was the same John Birch who, ever since he had been on the Army payroll, had been sending $150 per month back to his parents in Georgia, with instructions to use one-half of it themselves, towards making their lives a little easier, but to use the other seventy-five dollars per month to buy trees and plant them on any part of the family land which John might be able to call his own—or on land purchased for the purpose. Growing trees for the future not only represented to John a sound investment but, more important, a gesture to the adventure of life through the increase in living things. (Incidentally, his family followed his instructions faithfully and exactly. In order to make John's

34

money go as far as possible, his father and mother and brothers and sisters planted all the seedlings themselves, and those trees are still growing on land around Macon today.)

John's fianceé was a Red Cross nurse at the Yale-in-China hospital in Changsha. She was a devoted Christian, was well aware that John was all chaplain inside of his temporarily assumed warrior's shell, and was apparently content with the prospect of being a missionary's wife. For a little while John's letters home revealed some of the happiness he felt in telling about the girl he was going to marry when the war was over. In the first of these, a letter to his sister Betty, dated March 7, 1944, he wrote:

> Don't tell anybody else, because it's still a bit early, but I have found the girl I expect to make my wife. Her name is Audrey, a lovely Scotch girl in the British Red Cross, daughter of a Baptist missionary in the C.I.M. in North China. I think she loves me, and I *know* I love her.
>
> I love you, too!
John

But on May 16 he wrote Betty àgain, a long letter about many things, containing this paragraph:

> It's awfully nice of you to want to write Audrey a letter, and of course it wasn't "too early." Now, however, it is possibly a little late, since I have "busted" things up pretty thoroughly. She is a splendid capable girl, and I think both of you would be happy to have each other's friendship.

In letters to his parents he had already explained more fully, and with the pain showing more clearly between the lines. In one place he writes:

> Sorry for your sakes that Audrey's and my engagement is coming to naught, but I feel that it was contrary to the Lord's will to go on with it. I feel called to do some pioneer work in Central Asia after the war [he had long talked of extending his mission-

35

ary work to West China and even to Chinese Turkestan] and it will be no place for a woman, unless she be more consecrated than Audrey will ever be. It seems now that she entered so deeply into my heart that I'll never care for another woman, so I guess I'll return to my old creed. I Cor. 7!!

And in another letter:

Father, I am grateful to you, sir, for your wise and kind advice on marriage, happiness, and unselfishness. God has been very good to me, along with all your children, in giving me parents who love the right and the truth, and who have given us a knowledge of these, rather than treasures of silver and gold. Just now I feel especially unworthy and unprofitable as a son to such parents, since I have disappointed Audrey, and you as well. Now I can only ask Him who knows the innermost thoughts of our hearts, and yet loves us, to forgive my wavering. . . .

There are several more paragraphs about the broken engagement, in the two letters, mostly defending and praising Audrey. But they also make clear that no inner sacrifice or outside force is going to stand in the way of a determination to do his part towards offering Christianity, Christian ideals and Christian brotherhood to the people of China.

X

The Preacher Inside

BECAUSE JOHN's religious convictions were so deep, so simple, and so real, his attitude towards his own achievements and powers was a mixture of unusual modesty and of equally unusual assurance. He took little credit to himself for anything he accomplished, and always discounted its importance. But he put no limit to the possibilities of what a Divine Being might do through John Birch as one of that Being's worthy agents. To those of us whose religion is less fundamentalist in nature, it might seem that John gave too little credit to himself and too much to a Holy Spirit. But the distinction is of little importance. For John believed completely in free will, and even by his own understanding of the relationship of man to God, he had to be worthy in order to be chosen as one of God's instruments on earth.

He was entirely too human to be impervious to praise or gratitude. But he viewed both the deeds that brought on these rewards, and the rewards themselves, against too broad a background to let himself be deceived as to their significance. As he picked up commendations and honors, both Chinese and American, for his exploits in the field, he paused for the required moment to show has appreciation and pleasure at the recognition, and then turned his eyes resolutely ahead again. With regard to the Legion of Merit, awarded him on July 17, 1944, "for exceptionally meritorious conduct in performance of outstanding service" he wrote his mother at the end of a letter dated August 8:

A message from headquarters said that as soon as I return to the office the General is going to pin the Legion Of Merit medal on me. I think it's for a very ordinary job I did last fall which happened to attract the notice of my superiors. They ought not to cheapen the decoration by giving it when a man merely does his duty. I shall feel guilty in accepting this one. . . . Love, John

And on September 22, he wrote her again:

The General pinned the Legion Of Merit medal on me yesterday. The public relations officers took some pictures; I shall try to get a print for you. I don't deserve the decoration, but since they were foolish enough to give it to me I want you to have the pleasure of knowing I have it. . . . Love, John

37

This belittling of the honor probably contains about the normal quota of politeness and modesty. But the picture taken of John, as the medal is being pinned on him by General Chennault, is that of an "angry saint" concerned with the future, and not that of a pleased and flattered youngster gloating over the past.

With regard to his post-war plans, however, John felt a huge and inspired confidence—and a great longing to have the war over so that he could get on with the job. There was no doubt about his persuasiveness in the pulpit, or on any podium that might temporarily serve as a pulpit. For 2nd Lieutenant, then 1st Lieutenant, then Captain John M. Birch, Intelligence Officer, had never stopped preaching. There have been many stories written of fighting preachers, but John Birch presents the first clear-cut case I know about of the preaching fighter. While his military duties always came first, and the preaching always had to be both incidental and additional to military activities and movements, it is extremely doubtful if any full-time chaplain in China conducted more religious services or preached more sermons than John Birch during the three years John wore an army uniform.

This extra-curricular activity was carried on with not only the knowledge but the full approval of John's superior officers. He substituted for chaplains when requested, or took on assignments for which there were no chaplains available. He held services on Sundays, at Christmas, at Easter, and at all other proper occasions; in officers' quarters, in enlisted men's barracks, in official chapels or rented halls. He preached to the Chinese, civilian or military or both, whenever and wherever there was an opportunity. He preached repeatedly to audiences of many hundreds, and with equal earnestness to gatherings of a dozen or less.

Colonel Wilfred Smith has pretty well summed up the official attitude towards the missionary side, as distinguished from the more normal and obviously acceptable "chaplain" side, of those continued clerical activities.

"I think John's work as a missionary and the testimony he gave, a testimony which was not only a preaching but a living testimony, influenced the lives of more Chinese than he would have been able to reach if he had continued his normal missionary activities. . . . He was all over Central China. That one trip of three hundred miles [the same trek on foot to the Yangtze, to which we have referred before] John told me himself that he 'witnessed' in village after village. I told John he could, for I believed it would help his morale and it didn't hurt the work. . . . The fact that he had the freedom to give out the Gospel [tracts which John took with him whenever he could] made him more valuable in his military work. . . . The fact that John was a member of the Army and the Chinese knew he had been a missionary added to his prestige and gave him greater influence with the Chinese."

John himself was well aware of, and in full accord with, that last point. As he wrote his parents, the fact that he had been a missionary gave the Chinese more respect for him as an officer; but, more important, the fact that he was now a soldier and an officer, and was not being paid or supported in any way for his preaching, gave them greatly increased respect for his obviously voluntary missionary efforts. As the war wore on and on, the pressure and strain of his army duties became ever greater, and John himself inevitably became more fatigued throughout every fibre of mind and body, he felt for a while that he was losing some of his appeal and earnestness as a minister, and frequently condemned himself for failure to seize or make opportunities to preach the gospel. This seems to have been especially—and naturally—true at about the time he was breaking up his engagement. In his letter of May 7, 1944, to his parents, he writes: "I hope that God will give me yet further time to live for Him fruitfully here on this earth. I've wasted so much of His time already, living for self, that I really feel ashamed to ask for more!" But then he writes this paragraph:

One thing encourages me, however. When I was last in the Central China city where I met Audrey (this was after she went to

39

India), Rev. Lundberg, of the Evangelical Mission, asked me to preach in Chinese at his Young People's Service. I felt pretty low and unfit to help others spiritually, but agreed to anyway. The Lord graciously answered my prayer, and the service and message seemed definitely led and applied by the Holy Spirit. My own faith was renewed, too. I spoke on the 15th Chapter of I Corinthians, as it was soon after Easter.

Your loving son,
John

This seems to have been the turning point, in renewal both of faith in himself and of evangelical purpose. In a letter written to his sister sometime later, John summed up his intentions and his hopes, as to the part he would play in calling men to a Christian life "during the lust-ridden years which will follow this war." His fervor and his assurance both stand out in the following lines:

> . . . Often in these days I feel that those barren years are my apprenticeship, God-given, and that a message is being formed, by Him, within me, that will one day burn its way out and across man's barriers, into the souls of many men.
>
> I know that God is preparing me (has prepared, in some respects) to stand privation, pain, isolation, fatigue and physical danger. To what end? That I trust Him to show me in His own time.

XI

Commendations Without End

THERE IS a strong and universal tendency among human beings—among all races of human beings—to dislike the goody-good character. That John Birch was able completely to avoid this reaction is one of the most weighty items of evidence as to his strength and his promise. I have in my possession, today, official reports and letters and informal reports and transcriptions of verbal statements, literally dozens of them, some of them thousands of words long, from almost every American associated with him for as much as even a few weeks, during his whole five years in China. Many of these statements or reports were made long before John Birch's death, and without the remotest idea that they would ever serve as reference material for a biographical sketch of their subject. And yet nowhere is there the slightest suggestion or suspicion of distaste, because of John Birch's religious proclivity—or for any other reason. There is only universal liking and unrestrained admiration, at every turn. And the reason was that, as Napoleon said of Goethe, "here was a *man!*" Even those who did not share John's religious faith or enthusiasm (of whom there were several) were unstinted in their friendship, their cooperation, and their praise.

Many specific commendations of John Birch have been written or spoken by General Chennault. On one occasion he said that John was ". . . outstanding in devotion to duty. On several occasions he continued his duties in spite of serious illness. I learned on one occasion he was sick with malaria and I ordered him back to Kunming for treatment and rest. A sudden emergency occurred, he learned of it and came into my office. Though over the malaria he was still weak and should have had a month longer to recuperate, but he came and volunteered to go back into the area in Honan and establish communications again. It was when it looked as though the enemy would break through."

At another time Chennault wrote: ". . . John did a magnificent job with me. I always felt that he would do any job I gave him to do well and that he could be depended on to see things through. His loyalty to me personally and his devotion to duty was beyond anything that was expected of him. I cannot praise his work sufficiently." But Chennault really summed up all of the many grand things he said elsewhere in one line

41

he wrote about John Birch: "I have always felt towards him as a father might feel towards a son."

Colonel Wilfred J. Smith wrote officially of John Birch, on June 26, 1947: "At all times his courage, perseverance, and unflinching loyalty was an inspiration to American and Chinese personnel alike." On September 25, 1945, Major General Charles B. Stone sent a communication to the Chief of Staff in Washington, recommending John Birch for the Distinguished Service Cross. This communication, three typewritten pages, single spaced, was a carefully itemized and chronologically presented record of John's war service, from which we have already quoted. But it seems worth quoting further a typical summary paragraph, this one concerning the earlier part of the war:

> "Without any previous training in ground-air coordination, and with practically no guide materials or instruction, Birch, over a period of two years, during which he was almost continually in the field, living under the most primitive conditions and constantly in close proximity to the enemy, achieved phenomenal success."

On April 16, 1946, Brigadier General F. W. Evans wrote a long official letter to General Bissell concerning the military service of John Birch. From that letter let's also extract a typical paragraph, but this one concerning a much later period of the war:

> "From 25 May 1944 until the end of the war Captain Birch operated almost exclusively behind the lines. His duty was at all times extremely hazardous. Due to his outstanding ability in gathering intelligence and organizing intelligence nets he was an extremely valuable member of the Allied Forces and he contributed immeasurably in bringing the war in China to a successful conclusion."

More revealing than these official and semi-official eulogies of John's superiors, however, are many comments of his fellow officers. Captain James H. Hart, who served with Captain Birch behind Japanese lines in Anhwei Province, has written: "Where brave men were common, John was the bravest man I knew. . . . In civilian life I was a newspaper man and met many people but John Birch is the most notable person I ever had the pleasure to meet." Lt. Arthur Hopkins wrote of John Birch: "Without reservation I will say that he was the most brilliant, finest, most able, bravest officer I ever met." And another fellow officer, Edwin James, whom we have already quoted once, said simply of John: "I must confess he is the only living man on earth I ever worshipped." There are so many other similar experiences of affection and admiration that to catalogue them would simply wear out the patience of the reader.

Perhaps most important of all, however, was what the Chinese thought of this American in their midst. And we can gather unmistakable evidence in this respect from both 14th Airforce personnel and the Chinese themselves. Brigadier General Evans stated one reason that John Birch was such an outstanding intelligence officer was that he had so many Chinese friends behind the lines. That these were *earned* friends is clear from all sources. Captain Hart, in commenting on his own official recommendation of John Birch for the Congressional Medal of Honor, says: "John, however, erected his own monument in the hearts of the Chinese people. . . . Somehow, I feel that he is still walking the dike paths in China and still helping China's 'small person.' His name is legion there now, and I am sure will be ever green."

Colonel J. C. Williams has said that "no other American in China had a higher opinion of the Chinese, for whom he had done so much over the war years." And Captain Bryan P. Glass wrote: "John was a great favorite with the Chinese. Many of his Chinese friends, I am sure, would have been willing to have taken his place when the Communists assassinated him. John was a part of the great tradition established by the 14th Air Force and many Chinese, when hearing the name of the great force will think not only of Chennault, of whom they had heard, but of Pai Shang-wei whom they knew and loved."

Illustrative of the spirit of comradeship and the never-failing kindliness which won for John Birch this esteem of his Asiatic friends, and of the depth of their gratitude and friendship, are the following two letters. They have been copied verbatim, with no change in language, spelling, or punctuation.

Captain P. C. Wu,
Chinese Detachment,
AAFNS., SMAAF.,
San Marcos Texas,
May 2, 1944

Mrs. George S. Birch,
R. F. D. No. 1
Macon, Ga.

Dear Mrs. Birch,

Inclosed please find a Postal Money Order of $104.00 U.S., which I owed to your son, Captain J. M. Birch.

I had the pleasure to know Captain J. M. Birch back in Kunming, China. In fact, we worked together much of the time until I was assigned to United States sometime last year.

On February, I asked the favor of Captain J. M. Birch to send some money to my mother somewhere in the China southeastern seacoast owing to the fact that I could not send the money through the bank. Yesterday, I received his letter of April 21 saying that the money been remitted to my mother on April 20, and asking me to return the sum by sending you the equivalent amount.

I like to thank you for the kindness shown to me by your son, Captain J. M. Birch. He has been in China for long period, and always been good friend to Chinese people, and knows how to help them most. Had it not been for his obliging assistance, the transaction would not be possible. My mother and I owe much to you and to him. Thank you.

Your most sincerely,
[signed]   Pochen Wu
Captain, CAF.

44

Shanghai, China
January 9th, 1946

My dear Mrs. Birch:

I am a Korean who, in the past, has been a very best friend of your brave son late Capt. Birch on the battle field. I am now writing a few line accross the Pacific Ocean to the mother of a great soldier Birch. At the begining of a year I am once more to recollect my old memories.

Without an exaggeration your good son was a benefactor of Korea and China. Some time last February I had an opportunity of knowing him at Kumming while both of us were busy for the war activities. Soon after our meeting we became a pal. Through his good offices I had a great honor of meeting the Great General Chennault. Also I had a constant contact with OSS through his favor. His sacrificial help enabled us to have a successful independence movement of Korea against Japan. Not only among Koreans but also among Chinese the late Capt. Birch was so well known because his human elements which penetrated into the hearts of people. Even if our companionship was not so long, we shared tears and laughters together.

My dear Mrs. Birch, please don't feel so sad about your son's death. His sacrificial spirit helped to won the great war. Once more we are able to the world peace and security. Your good son fought not only for your great country but also for China and Korea. In other words he fought for the emancipation of the whole world from injustice and inhumanity. In commemoration of his deed the tomb stone was erected with the writings of "This is the tomb of U.S.A. Officer Birch who gave away his life for the liberation of China." His activities in China gave us a vision of lively demonstration of Christianity.

Please accept my admiration and love in your thoughts of your brave son. You gave us your beloved son for the restoration of the democracy in the world. The great and heroic death of your son and his personality will shine among us like the polar star.

May God bless you and your family forever.

I am,

Your son, late Capt. Birch's
best Korean friend

[signed]   Gen. Kim Hak Kyu

45

These Chinese (and Koreans) who knew and loved John Birch were not only thousands in number. They were geographically spread over hundreds of miles, from Kunming to Peiping, and they ranged from the lowliest coolies to the highest officials. Not General Chennault alone, but General Hsueh Yo and General Wang of the Chinese armies also clearly felt for John Birch the affection of a father for a son. And more important, perhaps, than the posthumous award to John of the *Order Of Cloud And Banner* by the Republic of China was the fact that the townspeople of Hsuchow dedicated a special cemetery for his above-ground vault, on a hill overlooking their city.

There was something about John Birch which inspired almost everybody to speak of him in poetic terms. One friend wrote: "The men of Chennault will tell you that, in Valhalla, the rafters rang when John walked in." A man who thought in terms of a pagan Valhalla was sure its slain heroes would still welcome and honor this fundamentalist preacher, who was so unflinching in his missionary zeal. So fully had John Birch lived up to all the standards of those heroes during his term on earth.

That term was pathetically short. This young patriot first put on the American Army uniform on July 4, 1942. He wore it with consummate distinction and consecration until the war was won and the Japanese surrendered on August 15, 1945. And only ten days later, while still wearing it, on an important, peaceful and official mission for his government, he was brutally murdered by the Chinese Communists.

XII

Captain Birch's Last Mission

IT IS DOUBTFUL if any nation ever had as much
trouble in giving up in a war it had lost, in surrendering to the
winner of that war on practically any terms the winner
wanted, as did the Japanese with us. As far back as February,
1945, at the time of the Yalta Conference, it was already well
known to our military leaders that Japan was ready to surrender. Long before the atomic bombs were even ready to be
used, the Japanese were trying, through the Russian inter-
mediaries in whom they put a tragically false trust, to reach
the American government with overtures for peace. And before the bombs were actually exploded at Hiroshima and
Nagasaki they were making frantic efforts to surrender. But
not until August 15 were they allowed to do so. For every
day that the war could be kept going meant further gains for
the Communists on the mainland of China, and a Japan more
demoralized and more vulnerable to Communist advances,
thievery, and infiltration. That the Communists were at that
time exerting sufficient influence in the very top councils of
our government to bring about such an incredible delay, and
to use such a barbaric means to further their ends, is now well
established by incontrovertible revelations of the past several
years. But few of the Japanese, who were then still officially
allied with Communist Russia through the Molotov-Matsuoka
Pact, and even fewer of the American people, had any knowledge of the way they were kept killing each other month after
month in order to serve Stalin's imperial purposes.

When General MacArthur sent President Roosevelt before
the Yalta meeting a memorandum[1] stating that Japan was al-

47

ready collapsing, that the Japanese were already making unofficial peace overtures, and that it would be folly at this stage to bribe Russia or even allow Russia to come into the Pacific War as our ally, Roosevelt brushed it aside with the wisecrack that MacArthur was our best general and our poorest politician. When Jacob Malik pigeonholed the actual Japanese offer to discuss surrender steps for more than two months, nobody in the White House or the State Department let on that they even had the slightest suspicion Japan could be licked without dropping atom bombs on their cities. And when, after Hiroshima had been destroyed on August 6, and the cries of Japan to surrender had become too direct and too widely audible to be ignored any longer, the stalling was still sufficient to allow Russia to get comfortably under the wire as a participant—and to begin immediately her "rush for Asia." But finally, nevertheless, on August 15, 1945 (in China, August 14 in America), the surrender was arranged and accepted.

This surrender did not clear up the problems in China overnight, by any means. For one thing, there were at that time three million Japanese, half of them in uniform, on Chinese soil. And the state of disorganization was so great, after eight years of China's war with Japan, and with all of these forces of the conquered enemy trapped on the land of the country they had invaded as conquerors, that many difficult missions were necessary to untangle the mess. One such mission, headed by Captain John Birch, started from an American airfield near Fowyang, in northern Anhwei Province, for Tsingtao, on the Shantung Peninsula, where there was a known pocket of disturbance. In the words of Colonel Paul L. E. Helliwell, John Birch was selected for that "particular mission because of his familiarity with the country and the language, and because of his superbly excellent relations with Nationalist and guerilla units operating in that area. The assignment was one of importance and was one on which I sent by far the best officer available." And Brigadier General Evans says that John "was sent on this mission because he was the only officer in that area who had a sound knowledge of that section of China."

That John himself considered the mission important is clear from the fact that he volunteered to lead it. For after three years of dangerous and difficult service, without any let-up whatsoever, John himself had admitted that he was about at the end of his rope, and had asked for a furlough. How significant was this request can be seen from the fact that John had continuously refused all previous offers of leave, despite the pleading letters from several members of his family in Georgia, and the pleas of even General Chennault himself. At one time, several months before, Chennault had insistently offered John thirty days leave in the States, with the customary free transportation provided both ways, and had kept the offer open for a long time. But John had turned this offer down, as he had several earlier opportunities, on the ground that his small service was still badly needed to help towards winning the war. Now he had actually asked for a leave, but then consented to have the request postponed until this one further mission, for which his special knowledge and abilities were so badly needed, should be completed.

Despite the fact that his commanding officers and John himself both considered the mission of great importance, however, its exact nature and purpose have never been revealed. For the War Department file on Captain John Birch is still classified as secret, and the information in it is unavailable to me or to the public. The reasons why it was originally so classified, by the Pentagon brass under Truman's thumb in 1945, will become fairly obvious later. But its continued classification today is apparently due to nothing more than inertia on the part of so heavy a body as the U. S. Army, and the unwillingness of any component of that body to stick his individual neck out and remove the classification barrier. For I have been told by one trustworthy friend who was privileged to see it—but not to reveal to me its contents—that there is absolutely nothing in that file, in his opinion, which could today endanger the United States or help any enemy in the slightest.

However, despite this "classified" hocus-pocus, and despite

the brazen misrepresentations perpetrated by the War Department in 1945 and its reports to John Birch's parents, and despite the deliberate obstacles raised to the uncovering of the exact circumstances of John Birch's death for years after that death occurred, the true facts with regard to all the main incidents of his last mission have now been well established. They are set forth below in reasonably full detail, but without any unnecessary elaboration.

When the party left Fowyang it consisted of Captain Grimes, Lt. Ogle, and Sergeant Meyers of the U. S. Army, Lt. Tung of the Chinese Army as liaison officer, five other Chinese and two Koreans, with Captain Birch as commanding officer. From the airfield near Fowyang they proceeded at first on horseback and then by boat, until they made contact, as arranged, with "puppet" authorities that had been working clandestinely for the Nationalist government. They then were taken by car to a village on the Lunghai Railroad, and stayed in this village from the evening of August 22 to the morning of August 24. At noon on the twenty-fourth they left by train, going eastward towards Hsuchow. At a point about fifty miles west of Hsuchow, where there was a station and a small Japanese garrison, they learned that there was a break in the track ahead. The engine went on, verified this break in the tracks, and came back. It was then agreed that John and his party would be taken by the engine and one coach up to the break, and be left there to proceed by foot towards their destination. This was done.

After the party got off the coach, Captain Birch and Lt. Ogle went into a small village nearby and engaged some coolies to help to carry their baggage. In this village they met a Portuguese priest, in charge of a Canadian mission, who gave them their first confirmation of rumors that Communists were making trouble in the area. Communist guerilla units had entered the village the night before and, besides doing other damage, had seized and carried away the mission's small stock of medical supplies. But it seemed unthinkable to John and his men that, being Americans, they had anything to fear from these

50

Communists, their allies in a war with Japan which had been brought to a victorious close only nine days before. Lt. Ogle has said, "we were feeling pretty good about the war being over"—undoubtedly a minor record-holder in understatements.

When Birch and Ogle went back, with this help they had rounded up, to the break in the railroad tracks, they found there, besides their own crew which had been left behind, a Japanese patrol which had been sent out to repair the line. This patrol supplied the American party with a handcar for its baggage. The party then proceeded a few hundred yards up the track, to another small station where there was a fairly large Japanese garrison. John made arrangements with them for his troupe to spend the night there. The Japanese were not inclined to fraternization, but showed a disciplined courtesy; and after routine explanations, they offered no objection to the Americans proceeding on their journey the next morning.

This was August 25, 1945. The party left the Japanese garrison about nine o'clock in the morning, various members taking turns pushing the handcar along the tracks. About noon they met up with a force of Communist guerillas, several hundred strong, some of whom were engaged in tearing down telephone wires. The guerillas identified themselves as attached to the 8th Route Army (the main armed body of Communists in China), but were not in any kind of military formation, although they were obviously taking orders from some leader.

The Communists, after stopping Captain Birch's troupe, also closed in on them from behind. But there were no wild shots, attempts to seize the baggage, nor threats of any kind. John went forward to talk to the man apparently in charge, and then went with him to see the chief commander. In about twenty minutes he came back, told his party that he had made arrangements for them to proceed, and the troupe went forward along the tracks again. As they did so, John told Lt. Ogle and his other subordinates of his conversations with the leaders of the Communist forces.

He had had considerable difficulty in seeing and identifying the officer in charge. (This unwillingness to disclose the source of top authority, in either their civilian or their military organizations, is an attitude so widely adopted by Communists everywhere as to be almost a reflex action with units of this size. The course serves not only to confuse and wear down anybody with whom they may be dealing, but renders any commitments that may be made more obviously non-binding and worthless as soon as they wish to disregard such commitments.) Either this officer or the second in command—John was not sure which—had demanded that the Americans turn over to the Communists all or part of their equipment. This John had refused point blank to do, explaining in plain language that his was a party of American soldiers on an official army mission, and in charge of American army equipment. His firmness had prevailed. Or so it seemed. What decision really had prevailed, and whether what happened later was on direct orders from the top leader of those Communist forces, will probably never be known and certainly can never be proved.

Captain Birch had been informed at the end of this conversation with the Communist leaders that there was another group further along the way, but that he would have no trouble with them. He was requested, however, to send Lt. Tung ahead, to explain the presence of the Americans, which was done. In a little over an hour the party met an outpost of this second Communist group. It consisted of only about half a dozen soldiers, behind a little raised place along the railroad tracks, who had the Americans covered with rifles and one machine gun when the party was ordered to halt. But Lt. Tung was right behind the soldiers, immediately stepped forward with two of them who may have been officers, and came forward to meet Captain Birch. Simultaneously, the soldiers fell out of their positions, and everybody felt obvious relief.

After a brief conversation between Captain Birch, Lt. Tung, and the two Communists, during which no sharp words or signs of unpleasantness were noted by the others, the four headed for the nearby village to talk to the officer in charge there. Before leaving, Captain Birch ordered Captain Grimes, Lt. Ogle, and the others all to remain with the baggage and the handcar. They pushed the car further up the track to a crossroad some fifty yards away. Sergeant Meyers went ahead to a small station a little further on and brought back another handcar. Lt. Ogle went to a courtyard nearby, to see if he could get some boiled water. The others, being able to buy some fruit, sat down to eat it. Numerous Chinese children had gathered around, and had helped in the pushing of the cars.

All of this peaceful waiting lasted about forty minutes. Nobody was concerned or alarmed, because the simplest negotiations always took considerable time in China, and there was no indication that Captain Birch had run into any kind of trouble. Then suddenly a large group of Communist soldiers came out of the village, set up a machine gun, and covered the whole party with rifles from two points. The officer in charge gave orders for the Chinese children to get away, and there were many other orders and shouts.

Lt. Ogle was in the courtyard at the time. When he saw a few Chinese civilians at the doorway turn with obvious concern and hurry into their dwellings he suspected trouble. Going to the courtyard doorway and looking out he could see that Captain Grimes and Sergeant Meyers were being disarmed. He learned later, from Grimes, that one of the Chinese in the party, as soon as he realized what was up, had stepped forward and said: "Don't shoot! Don't shoot! We will talk." The Communists had then swarmed down on the group and had taken Grimes' and Meyers' weapons. Lt. Ogle came out just as this was happening, and two Communists immediately approached to disarm him also. This he allowed them to do, on instructions shouted by Captain Grimes. Then the whole party was led into the village, lined up against a wall, and the hands of each man were tied behind his back. There were two Americans, eight Chinese, and two Koreans now left in the group.

In the meantime no word had come from, or about, Captain Birch or Lt. Tung. But in about fifteen minutes, while all

53

members of the party were kept lined up against the wall, were being stripped of their possessions, and were being forcibly restrained from talking to each other or to their captors, two shots were heard. Immediately after the shots it so happened that two American planes, P-51's, flew over the village. The Communists hastily led their captives northward out of the village, about a quarter of a mile, where they were kept for another fifteen minutes while the Communist detachment was apparently waiting for orders. Then the soldiers and their prisoners were marched away, in the direction of the Communist "capital" of Yenan, which they reached two months later. Eventually, the Americans had their possessions returned to them and were freed. Their deaths were not needed for propaganda purposes, and there was no point in tempting the supineness of the American government too far. The murder of Captain Birch, so widely known and loved all over Nationalist China, was sufficient.

XIII

A Hard Way to Die

WHEN CAPTAIN BIRCH and Lt. Tung, with the two Communists, left the handcar to go into the village, Captain Grimes and Lt. Ogle both insisted that they also should go along as a safety measure. But John apparently thought it would show more confidence and friendliness if he went without them, and preferred to make the negotiations alone on that basis. His orders, therefore, were for the others to stay with the baggage, as stated above. But Lt. Tung evidently was greatly concerned by what he had overheard of conversations among the Communists where they had last been stopped. As he and John found themselves being given a run around, on

CAPTAIN JOHN M. BIRCH, U.S.A.

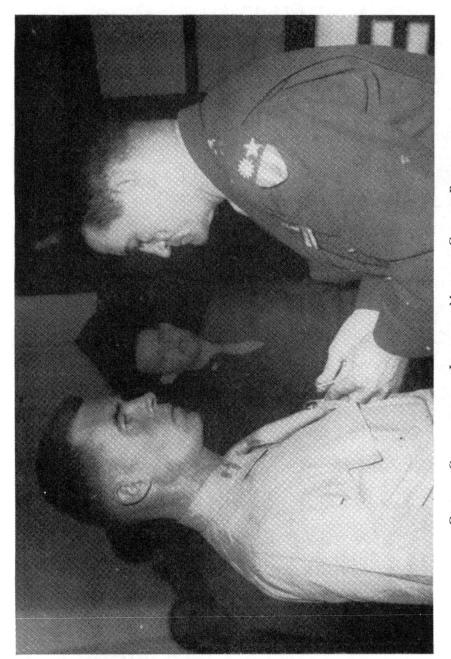

General Chennault pins Legion of Merit on Captain Birch.

John Birch (second from left) with Chinese and American comrades-in-arms.

Two days after the Japanese surrender and eight days before Captain Birch was murdered by the Communists. This photograph, taken at the "little outpost" mentioned in the text, contains the last known picture of Captain Birch. He is standing on the immediate left of the Chinese officer.

entering the village, and as the Communists kept stalling about taking them to the commanding officer or identifying anybody in charge, Lt. Tung frankly warned Captain Birch to turn back as his life was in danger. John's reply, as later quoted verbatim by Lt. Tung, was: "It doesn't make much difference what happens to me, but it is of utmost importance that my country learn now whether these people are friend or foe." He got a very clear answer to that question, which could have been of tremendous value to his country—and could have saved tens of thousands of other American boys, as well as literally millions of the Chinese whom he loved. He got it at the cost of an agonizing death. That his sacrifice was so completely in vain is one item of eternal disgrace to an administration which planned it that way.

We know that Captain Birch and Lt. Tung experienced approximately one hour of frustrating obstructionism, because that much time elapsed before the shots were heard. John argued continuously that he was in charge of an authorized mission of the United States Army, which the Communist forces, presumably our allies, should allow to proceed. Finally, in one group, which clearly contained one of the higher Communist officers of the locality, and probably the commanding officer himself, the leader ordered John disarmed. John naturally and properly demanded to know by what authority an American officer was being disarmed. As this had no effect, and a soldier moved forward to comply with the order, Lt. Tung intervened. He asked, if Captain Birch were to be disarmed, that he be allowed to do it. But as he was reaching for John's pistol—the only weapon John carried—somebody shouted, "No, shoot him first!" Whether this was the ostensible officer in charge, or whoever really had top authority in the group, or somebody else entirely, Lt. Tung never knew.

Two shots were fired. One caught Lt. Tung in the leg, he was also bayonetted, and he fainted as he was being dragged away. He knew that John was hit by the other bullet, but did not know where. The last thing Lt. Tung remembers was John saying "Wo pu nêng tsou la," meaning "I cannot walk

55

any more," when he was ordered to move, and the officer giving an order for them to be brought along anyway. Actually, John also had been shot in the leg; and that he really died of bayonet wounds was later established by the Chinese doctor who performed an autopsy between his two burials. The importance of this lies in the fact that, even if the shots had been fired by some excited soldier acting on his own wild impulse, such extensive bayonetting as John suffered could not have been inflicted without the direct orders or deliberate acquiescence of the officer in charge.

The Communist soldiers dragged the two wounded men, Captain Birch and Lt. Tung, to the side of an open pit on the edge of the village, and left them there to die, or as already dead. This was between two and three o'clock in the afternoon. Early that evening an old Chinese woman wandered past and said—to somebody, apparently a member of her family—"We had better bury these dead." Lt. Tung was just barely able to speak, and managed to get out: "I am not dead yet, please help me." The woman hurriedly told him to be quiet, as the Communists were still there. When they left, she said, she would come back and help. Later in the evening she did come back with help. They carried Lt. Tung to a shelter, and gave him what first aid they could.

The next morning a group of Japanese who came through the village recognized Lt. Tung as a member of the American party that had stayed with their detachment two nights before. They rushed him to a first aid station, and wired Hsuchow, giving all the information they had. Lt. Tung was then moved to a hospital in Hsuchow, and given the best treatment available in the command. Later he was transferred to the American Army Hospital in Chungking, for many months. Despite the loss of one eye and one leg his life was saved, and much of this account of the events of August 25 is taken verbatim from his testimony to various people.

When the old and kind Chinese woman came back with help late that evening, John Birch was already dead. Whether he had been dead when she first came near the bodies, or even when first left by the Communist soldiers, there is no way of knowing. Since he was beyond any help, he was buried near where he was found, by some Chinese farmers.

As is almost always true in China, word of the projected trip of the American mission had preceded them to Hsuchow, and the Chinese Nationalist forces there had been expecting the party for several days. When news of what had happened reached Hsuchow they immediately sent Col. Mah and some troops to Huang-Ko to question the local people. The farmers and townspeople took Col. Mah to Captain Birch's temporary grave, and Col. Mah's forces brought the body back to Hsuchow.

The day they got back Lt. Miller, an American officer of the Air Ground Aid Service who had known John in the field, also arrived. He took charge of the funeral, and Captain Birch was buried with full military honors. His body was wrapped in white silk and placed in a Chinese coffin. Missionaries and Chinese pastors of all the Christian churches in Hsuchow took part in the ceremony. The high ranking officers of both the Chinese and Japanese forces attended, and a guard of honor of twenty Chinese and twenty Japanese soldiers marched with the procession. The whole city was put in mourning.

John Birch was buried in a raised mausoleum, on a hillside on the outskirts of Hsuchow, overlooking the city. The site had been selected by Lt. Miller. General Ho, one of the two ranking Chinese officers present at the burial, raised a stone there to John's memory, with the inscription: "He died for righteousness." General Ho and General Tong, the other ranking officer of the area, told an official American investigator a little later that not only did they feel as if each had lost a close personal friend, but that they knew all China and the Chinese people had lost a good friend and a great supporter. This investigator wrote that the sincerity of their feeling was unmistakable. And at last report, many years ago—before Chinese Communist conquest of the area made all reports impossible—the burial place, with the body of another 14th Air Force man, Flight Officer Samuel Evans, in a vault next to that

57

of John Birch, had been made into a small park and was being beautifully cared for by the Chinese people of Hsuchow.

A Rupert Brooke might hopefully write that here was one small plateau on a hill in China which would remain forever American. Since desecration of the grave of such an American and such a symbol of America's great friendship for the Chinese people would be the most natural thing in the world for the Chinese Communists, that poetic hope is forlorn and unjustified. A more fitting epitaph from the poets, for this martyred hero who died so young, is the one already applied to him by Adeline Gray, a former instructor at Nankai University in China, who knew him well. She ended her own brief tribute to John Birch with these lines by Thomas Mordaunt, made famous by Sir Walter Scott:

> "One crowded hour of glorious life
> Is worth an age without a name."

XIV

The Hush, Hush Treatment

CONTRARY TO the impression perhaps occasionally created by the enthusiasm of this biographer, John Birch did not win China's war and our war with Japan, on the mainland of Asia, singlehanded. Although outstanding, by almost every standard of appraisal, he was still just one American soldier, with only the rank of captain at the end. Why was his story kept so carefully and completely from the American people?

That there was deliberate suppression of the news there can be no doubt. The only inkling of the event to reach America was that which seeped through from private sources. Constantine Brown, in his column of November 15, 1945, in the Washington Star, stated: "Long despatches are reaching Washington from Chungking and other tender spots in China. They are all marked top secret, although they deal with what is happening to the American soldiers and sailors in that area. None has yet been officially informed about the murder of Captain John Birch by the Chinese Communists." On November 16, 1945, Adeline Gray, who was herself a newspaper woman as well as a former instructor at Nankai, wrote John's parents that "had not the truth been suppressed, Captain Birch's death would have headlined every newspaper in the United States." And she later informed Mr. W. T. Anderson, Editor of the Macon Telegraph in John's home town, that "the murder was kept a 'hush, hush' affair, and no China correspondents were able to send out the story."

Again, there can be no doubt as to the deliberate misrepresentations by the War Department to John Birch's parents, concerning the cause and manner of his death; nor any doubt as to further and continued deliberate measures to block every effort of his parents to learn the truth. The essential accuracy of the account I have given of Captain Birch's death is beyond question. The impact of his personality and character had been so great that several of those who had known him in China set out to write books about his life. Events moved so rapidly that not one of them ever finished the job, but I have been the heir to much of the results of their labors. My information was gathered through the efforts of many people—not including myself—over many years, and verified at many points by the agreement of independent reports from different informants who didn't even know of each other's statements. And at least as early as September 20, 1945, the War Department's own internal information was headed:

Birch, John M.—Serial No. AC, 0-889028
Killed by Chinese Communists on the Lunghai Railroad
enroute to Hsuchow, China, on August 25, 1945.

59

But the War Department still persisted in its official report that Captain Birch had been killed by a stray bullet, without any mention of the Chinese Communists; and still found that it had "lost" or "misplaced" the addresses of officers who might be able to tell Mr. and Mrs. Birch the truth in or through Washington. It became obvious in time that the various underlings the Birches met were obeying orders or following a policy from above, the ultimate source of which these subordinates themselves probably did not know. The purposes of that policy, it became clear then, and is more unmistakably clear today, was to keep the fact that an American officer had been deliberately murdered by Chinese Communists from the American people.

Of course the truth was known all over China. It was to the advantage of the Communists to have their contempt for Americans and their lack of fear of any American reprisals widely known. They were profuse in their belated "official" apologies and explanations, for even these were so fantastic as to cause Americans to lose face by receiving them. Mao Tse-tung himself, for instance, solemnly offered the ridiculous assertion that the Communist troops had believed Captain Birch and the other Americans in his party were *Japanese in disguise*. One tricky corollary suggestion, flowing from this insolent tongue-in-cheek "apology," to be implanted in the minds of all who might hear or read of it, was that of course the Americans would agree there would be nothing to be upset about if it had been a Japanese who had been killed—even though we had signed an armistice with Japan ten days before the event!

We have no way of knowing from how high a source came the order to kill John Birch. It may even be that, contrary to the fears of Lt. Tung, no such order preceded Captain Birch to his last meeting with the Communists, and that the actual murder, by shot and bayonet, was the direct responsibility of only the detachment at Huang-Ko and of its commanding officer. But the resolution of this point would make little differ-

ence. For it is clear that the specific act was in accord
general policy, established at the top and well understoou
throughout the Communist forces.

Until ten days before then the Chinese Communists had
theoretically and supposedly been our allies, in our war against
another nation. What our relationship toward them was to
be now had become an entirely new and open question. The
first tangible answer, on the part of the Communists themselves, as to what their attitude was, and what they intended
the relationship to be, was given in the continuous pattern of
murder, capture, and torture of uniformed Americans in China
which began immediately. The deliberate and unjustified killing of John Birch, a captain in the American army on an official mission for our government, was—whether so intended or
not—the first overt act that established this pattern. It is clear
that the Communists, high and low, recognized John Birch
as standing for America, for Christianity, and as the very em-
bodiment of those qualities and forces which were in their
way. Whether "high" Communists specifically designated him
as an early victim matters little. For *some* Communists, high
or low, unquestionably implementing the known attitude and
desires of top leadership, liquidated this symbol of opposition
and provided this shining example of their power to liquidate
others who might oppose them.

As for punishing the individuals who committed the murder, there was never any slightest evidence offered of any
such punishment having been effected—or intended. To have
shown even any serious consideration of meting out punishment to the guilty parties would have weakened the propaganda value of the murder. Far from being punished, for all
we know, or insisted on knowing, the perpetrators of the deed
may have been given medals of honor. General Chennault has
stated: "If I had still been in China, there would have been a
squadron of B-25's blasting that Communist position with no
further questions asked." This would have been brutal retalia-
tion. But it is and was absolutely the only kind of language for

which the Communist murderers have the slightest respect; the only language that would have stopped them in their tracks and have prevented the *literally* millions of murders (about fourteen million according to authoritative estimates) that they have perpetrated since. And it was because Chennault understood this that he had been maneuvered out of the picture.

And so the net result was this tableau. The Chinese Communists murder in cold blood, without the slightest excuse, one of our most heroic officers: one of the best known and most widely loved by the Chinese people; and one of those most highly esteemed by Chiang Kai-shek's Nationalist Government—which even passed a decree of the Executive Yuan in his honor after his death. The Communists themselves don't care how widely it's known in Asia; they even keep the murdered man's companions, also Americans in the uniform of the American Army, as prisoners for several months, apparently to be sure that there can be no misunderstanding of their contemptuous attitude. But *we* go to extreme lengths to hush the whole thing up, for fear that it might "increase the instability in our relations with the Chinese Communists." As for an official demand from Washington that the murderers be punished, or be turned over to us for trial, or even that our captive soldiers be released, that couldn't be dreamed of—it might *really* annoy the Communists. The whole thing would be incredible, were it not so exactly of a piece with so many other acts and attitudes in our relations with these same Communists during this same period.

Why? The explanation becomes clear and convincing only when seen as just one manifestation of a broad purpose and powerful force sweeping almost all before it. The fourth of our five questions requires that our title be mentally amended to read: *The Life and Times of John Birch.* For it really hangs on the Times. To see this question, and its answer, in proper and revealing perspective, we have to look at least briefly at some related developments on the most sordid scene of American history.

XV

A Glance at the Times

JOHN BIRCH died on August 25, 1945. Keeping
that fixed point in mind as a central date, let's glance at what
else was happening in and to America—a few of the things—
within about two years on either side, or thus during about a
five-year period altogether. It's not a pleasant task. For although every separate item to which we call attention on this
scene has already been publicized many times, putting them
together in one montage makes all of the pieces more shock-
ing through their obvious relatedness to each other.

It was during these years that Lauchlin Currie sat in the
White House as a confidential assistant to the President of the
United States. Currie, a naturalized alien, has since been identified under oath as a Communist espionage agent. He denied
this under oath, and then fled the country. That he consistently labored and schemed on behalf of Communists and Communist purposes is beyond question. And Currie had as *his*
special assistant another alien, Michael Greenberg, a trained
Communist of long standing. Greenberg, who did not even
attempt to get naturalization papers, worked with Currie for
several years at the very center of American policy-making,
especially on the Far East; and used White House stationery—
as did Currie—to throw his weight around whenever it served
his purpose.

It was during these years that another Communist, Harry
Dexter White, prepared and put over the Morgenthau Plan
for the savage destruction of Germany; successfully promoted
our gift to Russia of our actual plates for printing occupation
currency which we had to redeem; held many high places in

63

our government where important day-to-day decisions were made, including at last the directorship of the International Monetary Fund; and—among his minor achievements—personally selected more than fifty of the appointees to positions of influence in our European occupation forces.

It was during these years that Harry Hopkins, the most intimate associate President Roosevelt had, used every ounce of his inside power and position, when necessary, to maintain a continuous secret shipment to Russia of all kinds of materials needed for an atomic bomb. This included 1465 pounds of uranium chemicals, most of which Hopkins helped the Russians to obtain from Canadian sources, and transship secretly through this country, when there were not one thousand pounds yet available for our own use in the whole United States.

But materials for experimentation and actual production of the bomb were not enough. Within this period Allan Nunn May and Klaus Fuchs and other spies turned over to their Communist masters all of our atomic secrets. And when Igor Gouzenko exposed to the Canadian authorities some startling glimpses of the incredible Soviet espionage activities on this continent, and McKenzie King went dutifully to Washington to alert our government, he was pooh-poohed into an embarrassed silence.

Within this period, in addition to the fantastic flow of supplies by air through Great Falls, Montana, we shipped eleven billion dollars worth of war matériel to Russia through the Red Sea route alone. But some sinister influences within the top echelon of our military hierarchy were powerful enough and clever enough to see that not even adequate ammunition reached either our forces or Chiang Kai-shek's forces in China. Even General Stilwell bitterly complained, "Bullets! My God, all we ask for is just bullets for our guns." (These same sinister forces were able to maintain this continued shortage of ammunition, even for our own troops, or for any troops in Asia that might use it against the Chinese Communists, right up to the time of General Van Fleet's complaint in the Korean

War.) And, as we have seen, one of John Birch's superior officers explained that one reason John was so effective in the field was that he was able to repair radios and keep them going when nobody else could; when, if just a tube got broken, it was all this officer's life was worth to get another tube.

During this time Franklin D. Roosevelt, President of the United States, was browbeating Churchill, deluding Chiang Kai-shek, deliberately lying to Mikolajczyk, hoodwinking Congress, frequently deceiving even members of his own cabinet, and making dupes of the American people, all on behalf of Stalin. Acting under the influence of Lauchlin Currie, Harry Hopkins, Alger Hiss, David Niles, his own vanity and an impulsive regard for his tragic "hunches," he gave Manchuria to the Communists, betrayed Poland into Soviet hands, and double-crossed fifty million European friends, who had fought with us faithfully against one tyranny, into the clutches of another one far worse. These are hard things to have to say about a president of our country. But such plain facts, completely proved, are both material and inescapably relevant to the theme of this biography.

(Also, the time has certainly come to stop pussyfooting around with ambiguous language about important truths of our recent history. It is not fun to point a finger at anybody. But when the evidence is beyond question, it's imperative now that we do point fingers at those who—whatever their misguided purposes or mistaken reasons—have helped to build up the power of our Soviet enemy in the past, are doing so at present, or seem clearly likely to do so in the future. In this particular case it is even more important that the facts be stated clearly, for the evidence is very strong that Franklin Roosevelt himself, in the final weeks before his death, came to realize what a dupe he had been, and what a danger he had created for his own country and other nations, by trying to satisfy Stalin's appetite at any cost, even of honor itself. It has taken us nearly ten years to catch up with what Roosevelt already probably knew, or at least surmised, on his deathbed. There is a procession of Soviet satellite states that now includes Estonia, Latvia, Lithuania, Albania, Bulgaria, Hungary, Roumania, Poland, Yugoslavia, Czechoslovakia, East Germany, China, North Korea, Tibet, and Guatemala.[2] Already on the shaky edge of being Soviet controlled are Italy, France, Iran, and two more of our southern neighbors in this hemisphere. If we ourselves, in due course, are not to become one in the same procession, we had better stop describing pitch black as off-color gray, or letting the Communists and their dupes and allies buffalo us into a futile silence about the "bygones" of past administrations.)

It was during this very year, of 1945, that there came into the presidency of the United States a man, Harry Truman, who had been selected for the job primarily through the influence of Sidney Hillman and of associates whom we now know to have been Communists. He had been first notified of his selection as the vice-presidential nominee, at a time when everybody except the American people knew Roosevelt was a dying man, by Sidney Hillman; at a breakfast-for-two arranged for that purpose. Properly to appraise the far-reaching effect of that development, it is necessary to remember how justifiably Mr. Truman boasts of extreme loyalty to his friends, without the slightest concern as to the character, background, or record of those friends. Truly and tragically, if Mr. Truman had literally taken orders from these original sponsors, and if they had in turn taken specific orders from Moscow, he could have done little more than he did anyway to block exposure of the Communists and their treasonous activities in our public life.

There are apologists for Harry Truman who try to distract attention from the great help his administration gave to the world-wide progress of Moscow-controlled Communism, by pointing to various offensives against Communist aggression he is supposed to have initiated. This is a biography of a young American hero, martyred by the Communists, not a historical survey of America's seven years under Truman. We cannot stop here to analyze the fallacious disclaimers of Communist influence during those seven years. But since the atmosphere of the period during which John Birch fought and died is very much a part of his story, it is worth while pausing long enough to scrutinize at least one of the arguments that Truman opposed Communist purposes whenever circumstances forced him to a clear-cut decision. Let's look at the chief exhibit of these Truman supporters, the decision to fight back in Korea.

The best way we can do this is to list certain completely established facts, and let the reader form his own conclusions. First, for several months before the North Koreans crossed the 38th Parallel, in June, 1950, we put ourselves and the South Koreans in the worst possible position to defend the bottom half of the peninsula against that attack. We announced to the world that South Korea was beyond our perimeter of defense, and visibly followed Owen Lattimore's advice to let all of Korea fall to the Communists "without making it look like we had pushed it." With the Russians known to be organizing and training a comparatively huge army of North Korean Communists, we restricted all armed forces of the South Koreans to a police unit of some fifteen thousand men. Despite money actually appropriated by Congress for the purpose, the administration somehow found ways to stall and delay so that no military equipment—not even sufficient ammunition—was sent to help the South Koreans prepare any defense. And we ostentatiously withdrew almost all of our armed forces from that part of Korea supposedly under our influence, without the slightest suggestion, much less insistence, that the Russians do the same with their forces in the north.

Then we deliberately ignored the most obvious evidences, the most convincingly detailed intelligence reports, of Communist intentions. In 1947 the Wedemeyer Report warned of what was going to happen in Korea—of exactly what did happen in 1950. Between June, 1949 and June, 1950 our army general headquarters agency in Korea sent to Washington 1195 consecutive warning reports, an average of three a day, as to what was taking place just above the 38th Parallel. The North Korean build-up, and its purport, were both unmistakable.

Yet, when the Communists did plunge across the line and invade South Korea, the administration claimed to be taken entirely by surprise. Actually, the only interested parties who were surprised, or at least who had any right to be surprised, were the American people.

Second, and more significant, was the supposed accident by which we got into this "police action." The United States did not declare war on Russia, or the Chinese Communists, or North Korea. *The United Nations* declared that Communist aggression in South Korea must be resisted, which was eventually translated into meaning that the United States should send the men, matériel, and money to maintain well over ninety per cent of this United Nations resistance. But the United Nations could not take any such action except through the Security Council, in which each nation had one vote—and any one of five nations had a complete veto power over any such action. Communist Russia was, of course, a member of the Security Council, and had this veto power. How did it happen, if the Kremlin did not actually want us to be fighting its Communist stooges in Korea, that Russia did not veto the decision? It had never hesitated to use this veto before, for the most visibly selfish purposes. To the Communist masters of slippery strategy, this problem was simplicity itself. A few months before the invasion of South Korea, the Russian member of the Security Council got himself ostensibly and noisily into an angry huff, over some ridiculously flimsy excuse, and stalked angrily out of the proceedings. He conveniently "kept his mad on" until after the vote had been taken to resist in South Korea. Then, as soon as barely enough time had elapsed to keep the trick from being too obvious, he got unruffled and returned to his seat in the Council. From then on the Russian Communists were very much a part of the United Nations higher command, directing this war against themselves in Korea, and with individual Russian Communists placed in positions of considerable importance in the actual conduct of operations.

Now if there is any one thing the conferences, diplomatic

maneuverings, and United Nations proceedings have taught us, over the past nine years, it is that the top agents of the Kremlin do not let their emotions interfere with their aims, or get piqued except by careful design for a definite purpose, or let any decision go against them by oversight or default. If our Army headquarters in Korea knew that the North Korean agents of the Kremlin were going to overrun South Korea—and they were shouting it to Washington at the top of their lungs—it is certain that Moscow's agent in the United Nations knew it. And to assume that he chose just that time, and that time only, to stay out of the Security Council, on an excuse that had been carefully contrived and was sheer poppycock, for any real reason except that Stalin wanted us to commit our armed forces to action in Korea, is to be naive to the point of absurdity.

Third, and most significant of all, we never did fight this war to win it, or allow our generals to do so. MacArthur, Van Fleet, Lt. General Almond, almost every general of importance who was in the operation, has stated unequivocally that on several different occasions, and despite the persistent hampering shortage of ammunition, we could have completely routed the enemy and won an overwhelming victory; and that on each occasion our forces were held back from doing so on specific orders from Washington. MacArthur, who wanted to win a war he was fighting or know how come, and who would have had enough prestige to force the issue, was removed from his command.

The Korean "police action" enabled the Communists to get a lot of experience in fighting American armed forces; to try out their planes and guns and other equipment in actual combat and familiarize themselves with ours; to use the peninsula as a rehearsal ground for the greater conflict whenever it might come. It got the American people accustomed to having their sons fight under the command and direction of the United Nations, with their objectives being determined by political manipulation and deals among the many nations, all voting with equal power, in the Security Council. It showed all Asia what devastation and misery would be wreaked on any country like South Korea that dared oppose the Communists and depend on the United States for help. It allowed a lot of Communist agents and sympathizers in America to strengthen their hands by going through the motions of a phony opposition to Communism. It gave the Communists a chance to convince millions of Asiatics—who could not know that we were fighting this war with both hands tied behind our backs—that in a military struggle the United States couldn't even beat the Chinese Communists. It enhanced the prestige and strengthened the hands of the Chinese Communists immensely. It added billions of dollars to the taxation load and the public debt of the American people, and pushed us that much further along the Marxian road of spending ourselves into bankruptcy. It enabled the Communists, by lying propaganda, to convince half the world that we had resorted to germ warfare, so that the reaction to their using it when the time comes will not be so disturbing to neutrals or even their own satellites who might still have any conscience left. It accomplished many other objectives of the Kremlin. And it did so without the slightest danger of the Communists suffering any harmful results other than the loss of a few hundred thousand lives, which meant no more to them than the lives of so many insects. For Stalin, in a moment of either rare boastfulness or of carefully calculated design, had convincingly implied to the Czech diplomat, Arnhost Heidrich, in 1947, that he had controlling influence inside the American Government. This influence, now immensely increased through the machinery of the United Nations, was sufficient to bring the war to a close at any time the Communists deemed a phony truce desirable.

Whatever else the Korean action may have been, its appraisal as an effort on the part of the Truman administration to oppose the real interests and purposes of Moscow requires a gullibility, and a blindness to the plain facts, that is almost beyond comprehension. As to most of the other moves made by Mr. Truman to thwart Communist aims, a careful analysis will reveal equally fatal flaws in the arguments of his apologists. Many of the arguments will be about on a par with the one that, after the FBI had insistently informed him that Harry Dexter White was a Communist spy, he promoted White to a more influential position in order to keep an eye on him.

XVI

More about the Atmosphere

BUT LET's return to our main theme. It was also during this same year of 1945, in fact during the very autumn of John Birch's death, that Patrick Hurley resigned as our ambassador to China. Finding our embassy in Chungking completely dominated, and all of his efforts at helping Chiang Kai-shek hamstrung, by Communist traitors and pro-Communist sympathizers among the "career men" in our State Department, he came home and let out a blast that should have rocked the country. But the Communists and their dupes and allies were too high up in our government and too firmly in control. They were able to smother Hurley's on-the-spot report of our betrayal of China as effectively as they were the on-the-spot report of Ambassador Lane, of our betrayal of Poland, two years later.

(It is completely certain that a huge majority of our "career men" and all other employees of the State Department, past and present, have been and are completely loyal and patriotic American Citizens. It is equally certain that the statements in the above paragraph are true, and that our course in Chungking and in post-war China generally was guided by a comparatively few traitors and their misguided dupes, who got themselves into sufficiently strategic positions to exercise enormous influence. But instead of worrying about the bad

71

smell given the whole Department by traitors, and helping to have these traitors exposed and thrown out, the career men and other employees and alumni of the State Department have continuously "got their backs up" at every charge of treason, no matter from what source—Ambassador Hurley, Ambassador Arthur Bliss Lane, Ambassador Hugh Gibson, just for instance—nor how convincingly documented. And this childish blindness and resentment, on the part of people who should know better, has been of infinite help to the traitors themselves in enabling them to keep on having their disastrous way in American Foreign Policy.)

It was during these years that George Catlett Marshall three times saved the Chinese Communist forces from probable annihilation by forcing three separate truces on Chiang Kai-shek; that he placed an embargo on the sale to the Chinese Nationalists of any military supplies, even bullets for their guns, at the very time when the Russians were arming the Chinese Communists out of the Japanese stockpiles seized in Manchuria—and boasted that he had disarmed thirty-nine anti-Communist divisions with a stroke of his pen; that he used his full influence to build the prestige of the Chinese Communists by repeatedly insisting—as spokesman for the United States—that Chiang accept and trust these murderers as partners in the government of China.

These were the years when the greatest American historian, Charles A. Beard, was disgracefully smeared into innocuous ineffectiveness, simply because he dared tell the carefully documented truth about what had been, and still was, taking place. When at least one editor of our official Army publication, "Stars and Stripes," in the Pacific Area, was a Communist agent. When a man born in Manchuria, educated in Soviet schools in Siberia, now using an assumed name, was caught with more than two hundred top-secret documents from Naval Intelligence and the State Department and other departments in his rooms—and was let off without even a fine. And when maps, blueprints, and miscellaneous documents of every kind, revealing in infinite detail every statistical, geographical, and physical fact of American life and power, went through Great Falls in a steady stream to Moscow, fifty black suitcases full at a time, under the cloak of diplomatic immunity.

These were the years when the magazine *Amerasia* was peddling the Communist falsehoods of T. A. Bisson and others like him as objective analyses. When the Institute of Pacific Relations, completely controlled and dominated by pro-Communists, was not only spewing its own malicious propaganda far and wide, but was serving as a tremendously effective employment agency for placing Communists and Communist sympathizers in our State Department. When UNRRA began channeling large shares of its huge funds through Communist agents in China, in Poland, and elsewhere. When we insisted that the supervision of our flow of Lend-Lease goods to Russia through the Middle East be handled by the very Communist agents who were stirring up hatred of the "American exploiters"; and when we ourselves thus supported the foundation of that Tudeh party in Iran which has made so much trouble for us—and for Iran—ever since.

It was during these years that the Office of War Information, under Elmer Davis as Director, became a veritable hotbed of Communists and Communist sympathizers. There was Lionel Canagata, calling himself Canada Lee, who became a radio narrator for OWI. There was Giuseppi Facci, who devoted most of his time to a Communist-front organization which was branded subversive by Attorney General Biddle. He was senior foreign-language information advisor for OWI. There was Raymond Juebzke, or Nicholas K. Ray, or whatever his real name was, who had actually been discharged from WPA, even in those easy-going days, for Communist activity. But this didn't deter Mr. Davis from making him one of the top press and radio program directors. There was David Stone Martin, an active Communist who solicited party memberships in his own home. He and his wife were both on the OWI staff. There was Rose Hanna, who had worked in Moscow, and was an active member of organizations officially cited by government agencies as subversive. *She was made chief re-*

73

searcher in charge of OWI's files on subversives! There was
Robin Kinkead, who would have been able to operate practically a whole Communist cell out of members of his own
family. His wife, his mother, and his father were all active
members of the Communist party. Mr. Kinkead's job was to
help prepare OWI scripts. There was Paul Keri, murderer, and
lieutenant of Bela Kun. *He was made the OWI's Hungarian
expert.* There was Piroska Halsz, who had also been active in
the Bela Kun terror. She was made a chief translator. There
was Lazar Herrman, now calling himself Leo Lania, who had
edited the Austrian Communist newspaper, *Red Flag;* and
John Terebessy, known to have been a former Communist
agent in the Balkans. They were both employed in the press
and radio division. There were Chew Sih Hong and Dr. Kung
Chuan Chi, whom Owen Lattimore (Mr. Davis' Pacific Area
Director of OWI) insisted, over the protest of an alert legal
advisor, that he wanted kept in the OWI even if they were
Communists. There were Julia Bazer, later a Fifth Amendment case, and Adam Tarn, who has since voluntarily become
a citizen of Communist-governed Poland. There were Herz,
and Arksy, and Balinska, three prominent employees of the
Polish branch of OWI, who later showed up in the service of
the Lublin Gang—Stalin's stooge government in Poland. There
was Annabelle Bucar who, after the war, went to Moscow, re-
nounced her American citizenship, and began writing scur-
rilous attacks on Americans. There were dozens and dozens
more, of practically all nationalities. There were, as James
Burnham has remarked, so many fellow travelers and "leftists"
that the identifiable Communists, although plentiful, were almost invisible behind them. And of course, in the very top
bracket, controlling the whole official flow of information
about China to the United States and about the United States
to China, was Owen Lattimore himself—with cooperation
available, when needed, from his good friend Joseph Barnes,
Deputy Director of OWI for the Atlantic Area.

During the years under discussion this crew and the whole

74

OWI, acting under the cloak of war-time secrecy and urgency, did almost anything it wished. A fair example of these activities was the beaming to China of its broadcast of articles published in Amerasia, and its circulation in China of the articles most critical of China that were published in this Communist periodical; or its broadcasts to Poland, which were labeled by the wartime Polish Ambassador to the United States as straight pro-Soviet propaganda.

It was during these years that the Office of Strategic Services, under Colonel (now Major General) William J. Donovan, so frequently threw the weight of American supplies, arms, money, and prestige behind the Communist terrorist organizations of Europe and Asia. Almost typical of the selections by Colonel Donovan of high-level personnel for this agency were the cases of Leonard Mins, Milton Wolff, and George Wuchinick. Mins, member of a well-known Communist family, himself trained in Moscow and in Communist-operated revolutionary schools elsewhere, a former officer in the Abraham Lincoln Brigade which had been organized by the Soviet secret police to promote Communist terror in the so-called Spanish Civil War—this man was given the job of gathering and analyzing information on the Soviet Union for the OSS. Wolff had been a commanding officer of the Abraham Lincoln Brigade when it had been recruiting gullible young American idealists to fight in the Communist butcher unit without letting them know it was a Soviet police instrument. When some of these young American dupes found out the truth in Spain, and rebelled against the Communist leadership, they were summarily executed. Wolff has since refused to state under oath whether or not he took part in these executions of American boys. But as a member of OSS he served as one of the most influential and trusted representatives of the American government in Italy during the war years. Wuchinick, also a graduate of the Abraham Lincoln Brigade, found the opportunity as a member of the OSS to work closely with Tito in Yugoslavia and with the Communists in China.

75

Then there was Maurice Halperin, who has been finally dropped in recent months, by a great and patient American university, for his preposterous juggling of the Fifth Amendment. He was chief of the Latin American Division of OSS. And there was Duncan Lee. Mr. Lee has denied under oath (in 1948) that he ever gave confidential information about the OSS to Communists or even knew that Elizabeth Bentley was a Communist. Miss Bentley has testified under oath that Duncan Lee had been a Communist party member who actually paid his party dues to her, and had been her most valuable source of secret information in the OSS. She stated substantially the same thing in her book, *Out of Bondage.* And J. Edgar Hoover, head of the FBI, has officially stated: "All information furnished by Miss Bentley, which was susceptible to check, has proved to be correct. She has been subject to the most searching of cross examinations, her testimony has been evaluated by juries and reviewed by the courts and has been found to be accurate." The reader will have to do his own guessing about the loyalty of Mr. Lee, and where it lay. But about one thing he doesn't have to guess, and that is the extremely important part played by Lee in the OSS organization. For Duncan Lee came directly out of Colonel Donovan's own law office, and was made his special and confidential assistant in managing the world-wide operations of the Office of Strategic Services.

There was David Zablodowsky, an admitted worker in the Communist underground. There were Leo M. Drozdoff, Jack Sargeant Harris, J. Julius Joseph, Irving Fajans, Paul V. Martineau, Carl Aldo Marzani, Philip O. Keeney, Irving Goldman, Helen B. Tenney, and others who all later became Fifth Amendment Pleaders. They all had jobs, and most of them important jobs, in this extremely sensitive and important agency. And serving as head of the China section of Research and Analysis in this organization was Professor John K. Fairbank—who says he isn't a Communist. Since he has been identified under oath as a Communist, but has denied under oath that he was, we shall have to let the matter rest there. But in view of his past actions and writings, he certainly ought to do, so far as the Kremlin is concerned, until a Communist comes along.

It was during these years that Communists and close fellow travelers infiltrated every important government agency; and pushed, pulled, and edged each other to very near the top in many of them. It would be easy to fill several pages with names of government employees who have since been shown to have put the welfare of Communist Russia above the welfare of their own country. (In fact, James Burnham has done so, in his remarkably good book, *The Web of Subversion.*) And when the war came to an end, in 1945, and so many of the wartime agencies were gradually liquidated, there was a great migration of these Communists and Communist sympathizers to the old-line agencies, such as the State Department, many of which—especially the State Department—were already badly infiltrated.

And finally, it was during these years that Dean Acheson climbed steadily to the top of our State Department, pushing out anti-Communists right and left as he climbed. In their place he brought in, and so surrounded himself with, Communists and Communist sympathizers, that on June 10, 1947 a Senate Appropriations Sub-committee addressed this then confidential memorandum (from which most names have been deleted, and which has already been published many times before) to the then Secretary of State, George Marshall:

CONFIDENTIAL

June 10, 1947
FROM: SENATE APPROPRIATIONS COMMITTEE
TO: SECRETARY OF STATE, GEORGE C. MARSHALL

It becomes necessary due to the gravity of the situation to call your attention to a condition that developed and still flourishes

77

in the State Department under the administration of Dean Acheson.

It is evident that there is a deliberate, calculated program being carried out not only to protect Communist personnel in high places, but to reduce security and intelligence protection to a nullity.

Regarding the much-publicized MARZANI case, the evidence brought out at his trial was well known to State Department officers, who ignored it and refused to act for a full year.

MARZANI and several other Department officials, with full knowledge of the State Department, and with Government time and money, promoted a scheme called PRESENTATIONS, INC., which contracted with a Communist dominated organization to disseminate propaganda.

Security objections to these and other even more dangerous developments were rebuffed by high administration officials; and there followed the substitution of unqualified men for these competent, highly respected personnel who theretofore held the intelligence and security assignments in the Department. The new chief of controls is a man utterly devoid of background and experience for the job, who is and at the time of his appointment was known to those who appointed him to be, a cousin and close associate of a suspected Soviet espionage agent. The next development was the refusal of the FBI, G-2, ONI and other federal investigative agencies to continue the whole hearted cooperation they had for years extended to the State Department.

On file in the Department is a copy of a preliminary report of the FBI on Soviet espionage activities in the United States, which involves a large number of State Department employees, some in high official positions. This report has been challenged and ignored by those charged with the responsibility of administering the Department with the apparent tacit approval of Mr. Acheson. Should this case break before the State Department acts, it will be a national disgrace.

Voluminous files are on hand in the Department proving the connection of the State Department employes and officials with this Soviet espionage ring. Despite this, only two persons, one of whom is MARZANI, were released under the McCarran rider because of their subversive activity.

1. ————————	6. ————————
2. ——————	7. ———————
3. ———————	8. ————————
4. ————	9. ————————
5. ————————	

are only a few of the hundreds now employed in varying capacities who are protected and allowed to remain despite the fact that their presence is an obvious hazard to national security. There is also the extensive employment in highly classified position of admitted homosexuals, who are historically known to be security risks.

The War and Navy Departments have been thwarted for a year in their efforts to carry out the German Scientist program. They are blocked by one man in the State Department, a protege of Acheson named ——————, who is also the chief instrument in the subverting of the over-all security program.

This deplorable condition runs all the way up and down the line. Assistant Secretary ———— also surrounded himself with men like ———— and with —————— who has a notorious international reputation. The network also extends into the office of Assistant Secretary ————.

SUBCOMMITTEE OF
SENATE APPROPRIATIONS COMMITTEE

And these were the years when a communication of such a nature, from such a source, brought absolutely no action, interest, nor even visible attention. The Communists, their dupes, and allies had been able to rise so high in our government, to become so influential, that they could brush off charges like this without even missing a stroke in their subversive activities.

79

XVII

How Did It Come About?

TIME AND room for a more complete delineation
of the web of subversion would remove any surprise on the
part of a reader that the story of John Birch had been carefully suppressed. The interlocking cooperation by Communists and their dupes and allies, to slant all efforts, actions, and
information towards helping the Communist cause, and to
elminate or play down every item of unfavorable truth, was
so widespread, so powerful, and so skillfully conducted behind the scenes, that getting the life and death of John Birch
ignored was merely a minor chore. It was at this very time
that this same conspiratorial group succeeded in convincing
the American people, or enough of us to serve their needs, that
Mao Tse-tung, Chou En-lai, and the other murdering tyrants
in this particular advance troop of the Kremlin, were agrarian
reformers and really good democrats at heart. And it was within the period we are talking about that they were powerful
enough, and extended their fingers of control high enough in
our government, to have the official report of General Wedemeyer on the true China situation completely suppressed, by
the recommendation of George Catlett Marshall and the specific agreement of Harry Truman. In the midst of such epic
achievements the little matter of keeping Captain Birch's
murder out of the news was so easy and natural as almost to
be automatic.

The real question then, even in a biography of John Birch,
and in approaching all surrounding matters as the setting in
which his purposeful life and tragic death occurred, is this:
How did such a conspiratorial group of Communists, dupes,

and allies ever get such tremendous direct power and far-reaching indirect influence in our government and throughout our nation?

To give the complete answer to that question we should have to go back to the days in the 1930's when it was fashionable for almost everybody in Washington to express admiration for the "Soviet Experiment" and to vie with each other for the friendship of its representatives. When so personally foul a character as Oumansky, various parts of whose foulness from larceny to murder were public knowledge, could be and actually was treated with marked respect and even subservience by the most important representatives of this nation, because he was a Soviet "diplomat." When Earl Browder, head of the Communist party in the United States, had the run of the White House for years, and actually directed—from the White House—operations in 1938 to purge senators who had opposed the court-packing scheme in 1937. When both Franklin D. Roosevelt and John L. Lewis were sure they could "use" the Communists to support their own purposes and then discard them at will.

We should have to go back further. To 1934, when Frances Perkins and Henry Morgenthau and Henry Wallace persuaded President Roosevelt to have us join—and begin largely financing—that great organized conspiracy to socialize all the nations of the world, the (deliberately misnamed) International Labor Organization. To the hordes of ILO members, from Montreal and London and Geneva, who flocked to Washington, found themselves comfortable nests inside our government payroll, and began so energetically—and ably and slyly—creating a collectivist atmosphere in which communist doctrine could thrive. To 1933, when Henry Morgenthau and a young lawyer named Dean Acheson were so instrumental in getting the United States officially to recognize that government and establish diplomatic relations with Moscow. When the great influx of Communist propagandists, organizers, saboteurs, and spies began, before the ink was even dry on their solemn promise that they would not thus abuse our hospitality.

And further back, to 1921, and the transformation of the old Intercollegiate Socialist Society into the League for Industrial Democracy. This league, of which leading lights over the next decade were Robert Morss Lovett, Charles P. Steinmetz, Norman Thomas, Harry W. Laidler, Stuart Chase, Paul R. Porter, Paul Blanshard, Louis Budenz, and John Dewey, had one specific purpose and reason for existence. This was "education for a new social order based on production for use and not for profit." *Production for use and not for profit* is, of course, at the very center of Marxian doctrine, and the League carried out its educational program with considerable success. For in 1933, when Roosevelt looked around for the generals and colonels and corporals to lead his army of "social change," the League for Industrial Democracy had 5,652 members as the greatest single source of these administrators and advocates of the new order. (Roosevelt called it the "New Deal," but the German and British Socialists had called it by such names as the "New Order" or the "New Course"; and most of these converts were well aware, even if the American people were not, that it was exactly the same program.)

And yet further back. To 1905, when the Intercollegiate Socialist Society, which was later to become this League for Industrial Democracy, was itself formed, in a loft at 140 Fulton Street, New York. Among the sophomoric young idealists who founded the society were Upton Sinclair, Clarence Darrow, Jack London, Morris Hillquit, and Owen R. Lovejoy. The organization of chapters began at once, and was carried on so energetically that by 1912 there were forty-four such chapters in that many different colleges. Among the early presidents of local chapters were Walter Lippman at Harvard, David J. Saposs at Wisconsin, Frieda Kirchwey at Barnard, and Walter Reuther at Wayne. Prominently active in other chapters, in the years before the first World War, were Bruce Bliven at Stamford, Vida Scudder at Wellesley, Alexander Trachtenberg at Trinity, John Spargo at Amherst Agricultural, and Eugene V. Debs at Columbia. Other leaders in early stages of the movement included Ordway Tead, Alexander Meiklejohn, Isador Lubin, William Shirer, Paul H. Douglas, Vladimir Karapetoff, Heywood Broun, Lewis Gannett, and Broadus Mitchell. Among those acting as organizers, or as writers and lecturers to help the organization along, were Ella Reeves Bloor, Frances E. Perkins, Lincoln Steffens, Rose Pastor Stokes, Victor L. Berger, Bouck White, W.E.B. DuBois, Scott Nearing, John Haynes Holmes, Roger M. Baldwin, Frederick Vanderbilt Field, Felix Frankfurter, Joseph P. Lash, Max Lerner, J. B. Matthews, Nathaniel Peffer, Victor Reuther, Anna Louise Strong, Jerry Voorhis, and James A. Wechsler. Here are found many of the names of those who deliberately set out to make America over, into the pattern of a socialist-Marxist state, as had been envisaged for Germany by university students and professors, the radical theorists, and the class-hatred boys of Bismarck's day—and as their cousins in the Fabian Society of England were already doing for that nation half a generation ahead of them. Keeping in touch with the theories, methods, and successful experiences of the German and British leaders of socialist thought and action was a most important function of these American collegiate organizations.

And earlier still. To Germany of the 1880's when Bismarck and later William II were stealing the thunder of the rising Marxist storm, and cleverly using it to build a central government with more detailed power and minute controls over the lives of its subjects than had been seen since the time of Constantine. When Adolph Wagner and his associates were crystallizing the nebulous theories and generalities of socialism into its infinitely intricate and opportunistic legislative pieces. When the practical planners were proving that socialism, instead of being willingly and consciously assumed by the masses as a desirable condition of life, was something to be imposed on a people from the top; and were gradually accepting the inevitable corollary that a descending hierarchy of government agents, to force this socialistic organization of society on the people for their own good, was justified if necessary. When the pattern of *state socialism* was being set for all the world to follow for a hundred years.

And further back yet. To the fulminations of Karl Marx and the elucidations of Friedrich Engels. To the writings of John Stuart Mill and Jeremy Bentham and Robert Owen. To the widespread promulgation of that fundamental concept of all socialist idealism, "the greatest good of the greatest number." We should have to go back to the very beginning—in modern times—of that incredible assurance, on the part of an increasing number of sociological geniuses and experts, that they *knew*, beyond all possibility of doubt or error, what was best for their more ignorant fellow-humans and what would actually result in "the greatest good for the greatest number." To the beginning of that militant determination on the part of these self-appointed demi-gods, basking in the delightful glow of their own infallibility, to use *any* means to force governments and peoples into the mold designed and being built by themselves. To the last beginning of this recurrent pathological cyst in the philogenetic case history of the human mind.

We should have to trace the gradual growth of this cyst, of omniscient tyrannical altruism, as it developed in three generations to the point that the noblest idealists have been willing—are still willing—to resort unhesitatingly to perjury and murder and treason to foist their ideas upon the world. To give the full story of the spread and deepening of this obsession we should have to write a hundred books of a thousand pages each. And that is obviously beyond our purpose, or ability.

We can point out, however, that these "infallibles" close their eyes to many easily discernible facts. One is that the institutions of civilized man, his sociological machinery, cannot long survive or function creatively when inundated by the flood of collectivism. Historical experience has proved this beyond question, with regard to human social units of every size and circumstance; from Robert Owen's New Harmony experiment on a fertile pioneer front, to the great Roman Em-

84

pire of the West with all of its accumulated urban and com-
mercial advantages, to the middle-sized city state of Sparta at
the very height of its ascetic virility. But the disciples of Mill
and Marx and MacDonald are afraid to look at this historical
evidence. Even to glance at such ruins might cause the glitter-
ing mirage, on which they are focussing with such hypnotic
concentration, to lose some of its brilliance or even to begin
to fade away. On the beauty and the reality of this mirage
they are willing to gamble high stakes indeed; to gamble on
causing the starvation, torture, or prolonged suffering of still
more hundreds of millions of their fellow human beings; to
gamble on causing, or hastening, the suicide of a civilization;
to gamble on two even more far-reaching catastrophes which
we'll discuss in the final section of this book. To such people
the murder of John Birch would have seemed an inconse-
quential trifle in this gamble for Elysium, even if they had
known such a heroic individual—and opponent—ever existed.

XVIII

The Opposing Forces

OUR FIFTH and last question was: What is the significance of the life and death of John Birch? That question
involves deep and fundamental premises as to the significance
of any individual human existence. But this is not a book of
philosophy, and we cannot pause here for a study of man's
relation to cosmological purpose. Keeping our inquiry, therefore, within the narrower limits that were intended and are
appropriate, we might restate it this way: What is there about
the life of John Birch, except for its human-interest value, that
justifies a formal biography? If the reader will bear with us,
we'd like to approach this question along several different

85

lines of thought. They all converge to place this young man at a focal point of a physical and ideological struggle far greater and more important than has even yet been generally realized. And here, too, we can hope that the answer will gradually become both clear and convincing as we thus consider the forces which he so faithfully represented and those to which his whole outlook was so unalterably opposed.

For John Birch personified everything that the Communists hate. First, he was not only an American, he was one of the finest examples of Americanism, in all the traditional meaning and promise of that unique term. He lived and worked and fought and died, always literally giving the best that was in him, to strengthen those principles and beliefs which had brought human evolutionary and spiritual progress to its high-water mark in the America he inherited.

There was poverty in that America. Sometimes it was grueling and widespread poverty. John Birch had lived through it and knew it well. But John also knew, both intuitively and from actual observation, the difference between poverty in America and poverty in other lands. The ceaseless gnawing hunger accepted as commonplace in huge parts of China was rare indeed in this country, and actual famine completely unknown. Nor was hunger ever deliberately imposed on any segment of the American people, by government for its own ends. The brutal and literal starvation of three million Ukrainian kulaks by Stalin, on their own self-sufficient land, and simply because they resisted collectivization of that land, occurred at the same time as the worst of our depression of the thirties. But the like of any such catastrophe in this country was so little to be feared, or even imagined, that this Kremlin-contrived mass murder could not even be believed until the evidence and revelations became overwhelmingly conclusive.

Poverty is something which the Communists everywhere try to exploit. But poverty in America produced no bitterness, in men like John Birch, towards their government or towards their fellow men. For there was always freedom to move, to try, to hope and plan, to pit oneself against economic rather than governmental forces; to struggle against poverty as an individual or family responsibility, rather than as something imposed by the errors or ambitions of a tyrannical state and thus beyond the power of the individual to do anything about. An individual could enter that struggle with a justified American assurance that work and self-denial and thrift would bring better days in time; that while the boat of his own destiny was sailing in temporarily rough waters, he was still, under God, the captain of that boat and the master of his own fate.

John Birch had been through all the experiences of America's worst economic travail, without losing any of his preference for the American economic and political system to those that other countries had to offer. He had not become in the slightest susceptible to the doctrine that it is either the duty of the state to order the lives of its citizens, or within the power of the state to provide for them better than they can do it for themselves. A "prose poem" which he wrote in April, 1945, contained this sentence: "I want of government only protection against the violence and injustices of evil or selfish men." And this characteristic of Americanism is one which makes the Communists boil with frustrated rage.

There was pacifism in America, and internationalism, and distrust of the political purposes and honesty of our own government. These were attitudes which the Communists intended to exploit to the fullest. The freedom to criticize and disagree among ourselves had torn us widely apart. The Communists knew, better than anybody else, to what ends they would go and what means they would use to sow even greater dissension among us in the years after World War II. There could not be the slightest question, however, that John Birch would maintain an unshakable and heroic loyalty to America, in whatever cold wars or hot wars might arise with any foreign power. And a loyalty to one's own country, that cannot be weakened or divided even by allegiance to the noblest ideals of human brotherhood, much less by the phony parade of the shells of such ideals for the promotion of a tyrant's aims—such a loyalty, while still by no means exclusive to America, is another characteristic of classic Americanism which the Communists hate as a mole hates the daylight.

It is a tenet of Americanism that the right to own private property must not be abridged. It is a widely held conviction among Americans that their economic freedom is inseparably intertwined with their political freedom and their personal freedom in all other activities. They recognize, more by instinct from their pioneer past than by knowledge of how completely their feeling is supported by historical experience, that any chipping away of their economic freedoms, however insidiously done by governmental forces, means a surrender of other rights as well. The Communists, aware that economic freedoms are the most vulnerable of all to demagogic attack, and aware of the inevitable consequences of their destruction, have turned loose every propaganda device in their arsenal to batter down this characteristic of the American philosophy. But with John Birch they could never have made the slightest impression. In that same "prose poem" we have already quoted, John had his "war weary farmer" say: "I want some fields and hills, woodlands and streams, that I can call my own." Although determined on a career of ascetic dedication for himself, he had a fundamental American respect for the desire to own property, and for the proper place of this desire in a civilization of free individuals, that no amount of Communist sophistry would ever have been able to shake. A man who takes that half of his salary that he retains for himself, and invests it in barren land and in young trees to be planted on that land, to make it no longer barren—such a man is no prospect, not even a remote possibility, for the siren salesmen of Marxian revolution.

Next to the individual himself, the unit of responsibility and the basis of reciprocal dependence in America is the family. Our society is an organized purposeful entity, of which the millions of families are the sustaining cells. There is nothing unique to America in this characteristic. Extremely strong family ties have been a notable part of the pattern of social organization in many countries. But this tremendously pow-

88

erful family relationship between individuals is something which the Communists have been compelled to wear away by abrasion and practically to destroy altogether, before they could convert enough of the individuals of these families into willing slaves and worshippers of the state. Not only have the Communists debased both the ritual and the significance of marriage, in every country that they have controlled long enough; not only have they tried to make children at an early age look to the state, rather than to their parents, as the purveyor of necessities and the guardian of their well being; not only have they deliberately torn families apart by the millions; they have committed a far greater crime than any of these, by overpowering, with their specious indoctrinations, one of the noblest and most deeprooted instincts of man. For the Communists have successfully achieved the willing betrayal of parents by their children, and of children by their parents, for nothing more reprehensible than a lack of enthusiasm for a slave state. They have done this on a widespread basis, always on the grounds of a starry-eyed idealism that cannot admit the possibility of its own error, and as an important part of the Communist means of stamping out all opposition to its régime, of the present or of the future.

But for Americans of John Birch's background, of his love for his parents that amounted almost to reverence, of his deep and glowing affection for his brothers and sisters that shines out so continuously in his many letters to them, of his memories of their poverty and struggles and pleasures and sorrows and proud moments together; for him any Communist effort to tear down this idyllic attachment to a family hearth would have been absurdly futile. A man who, wishing to own forested land for his own future security, still takes one-half of his officer's salary (the first appreciable income he had ever had) and sends it gladly every month to his parents for the remaining three years of his young life, to make their living a little easier—the persuasion of such a man to substitute loyalty to the parenthood of the state for loyalty to the human parents he revered and admired would have been beyond

89

even the Communists' most clever and patient cunning. Sons like John Birch were, and would remain, insuperable stumbling blocks to the Communists' most insidious attacks on American family life.

Americanism is not completely definable, of course. And even of those prejudices, beliefs, and traits of character which most observers would accept as components of Americanism, there are many about which there would be strong differences of opinion as to whether they called for praise or censure. But when the doubtful or controversial characteristics are winnowed out, and only the noblest moral, political, and traditional values are left, out of that total environment for human life and human happiness which we inherited, we reach two parallel and irrefutable conclusions. One is, that John Birch embodied the best of those values. And the second is, those are exactly the values and ideals the Communists hate most, as obstacles to their conquest of America and enslavement of the world.

But there are *two* great bulwarks still in the way of this Communist ambition. One is a political entity, the United States of America. Other countries are resisting Communism, of course. But it is the productive strength of America and the ideological strength of Americanism that form the core of this military and political resistance.

The other great bulwark is the organized power of the Christian religion. Here too, other religious faiths—the Jewish and the Moslem followings, in particular—are doing much to oppose the Communist advances. But it is the greater numerical and material strength of Christianity, and the complete irreconcilability of Christian ideals with Communist methods and purposes, that form the core of this spiritual resistance.

And it so happened that John Birch represented each of these anti-Communist forces with equal honor and faithfulness. To him Christianity was no vague obbligato of half-defined doctrines to which one paid lip service, and of discomforting moral precepts which merely kept an elastic conscience from stretching too far. It was a dynamic faith, which pointed the way through humility, brotherhood, and righteousness to a better world composed of more noble human beings.

Many of us today cannot share the simple and fundamental faith which moved John Birch to such a self-sacrificing life of service to his fellow-men, and caused him to project for himself an even more single-minded devotion to the service of his God and of humanity in the years to come. But those of us who have not lost all sense of gratitude to the saints and martyrs, the teachers and poets, the heroes and dreamers, the workers and inventors, the good men and wise, who slowly and painfully created for us that predominantly Christian civilization which we inherited—we do share with John Birch a number of cardinal beliefs which are ties that bind together men of good will throughout the world. And these are the very beliefs, of man about his spiritual nature, that the Communists know they must overcome before they can substitute therefor the pseudo-religion of Communism.

One is exactly that right, of any human being, to believe what he wishes about his own relations to God, and to worship any Divine Being to the extent and in the manner dictated by his own belief and his own conscience. We simplify this great principle by the word *tolerance*. And while almost all religious groups have practised cruel intolerance at some time in the past, we have all learned over the centuries—Jews, Christians, Moslems, and others alike—that tolerance is an important manifestation of a great spiritual tenet common to us all: "Do unto others as you would have them do unto you." Today only the Communists have reverted to that principle, of the dark ages of religions and of civilizations: "Destroy your enemy's gods, and force him by the sword to worship yours."

It happens that John Birch, in the ardent certainty and fervor of his own early faith, had been guilty of intolerance— or of what might be so construed by many people. He was too kind and too civilized a Christian, even in those days, ever to have carried this intolerance to the point of cruelty to another human being or oppression of another faith. But he believed

91

that a man who had been hired, by a particular group of a particular religious persuasion, to teach and preach their beliefs to their sons and daughters, had no right to use his position to preach opposing doctrines. And at Mercer he had conducted quite a militant campaign in support of this point of view.

But it is doubtful if, by the time he reached China as a missionary, John would have felt that, in religious matters, even this course of action was justified or wise. He had learned to lean entirely on the power of persuasion, and on a sublime confidence that the truth as he saw it would ultimately prevail. Just how tolerant, in spirit as well as in action, John had become, is revealed by one development incidental to his war service. It is a development in the recital of which we must tread on tender ground. For in the southeastern states, where John was raised, there were almost no Catholics. For this reason a prejudice against Catholics, growing out of ancestral traditions and reasons that were themselves largely forgotten, had been transmitted and strengthened from generation to generation, through lack of any direct contact with objects of that bias which might soften it, until the prejudice had become both strong and almost universal. Just how strong the feeling was, at the very time John Birch was a growing boy in the South, became a matter of record when such staunchly Democratic states as North Carolina and Virginia went for Herbert Hoover in the 1928 presidential election, rather than accept the Catholic, Al Smith, as their candidate. There is no doubt that, to a fundamentalist Protestant like John Birch, it was actually much harder to see goodness in a Catholic than in a Jew or even a Moslem. The attitude of tolerance, friendship, and cooperation which John acquired towards Catholics, even Catholic priests, during his experiences in China, therefore, redounds greatly to his credit and to theirs.

There are many witnesses to this attitude, but one will suffice. Here are the exact words of Colonel Wilfred Smith, repetitious but revealing:

"The thing I liked about John was that although he was a very fervent Christian, he was also a very fine soldier. He reconciled the work he was doing in the Army with his burning missionary zeal and a strong feeling that China would have to be freed from the Jap menace before missionary work could be started again. We had two or three Catholic officers. One day John came to me and said, 'I have learned something. I find I can respect the Catholics. I have learned they can be gentlemen. We do not have many Catholics down south, and I have learned something. I have learned from my experience that Christianity is something from the heart. When I was ordained and came out I did not think that was possible.' John matured in his Christian experience. I saw him develop and change from a rather naive approach to one of maturity. It was very evident in the tolerance which he was able to feel toward Christians of other denominations than his own. I first knew John as a Southern Baptist, but John said that Christian fellowship was possible with anyone from the heart and not from denomination. It used to amuse me but without any kidding or urging he volunteered that information. He changed from a boy to a man."

The Communists, in their war to the finish on all religion, as in all of their other strategic drives, have left no tactical stone unturned in their conduct of that war. They have systematically stamped out religious observances and destroyed or taken over religious meeting places; they have consistently reviled, persecuted, and murdered religious leaders; and they have attempted to eliminate every religious hold on the mind of the young—except for always temporary concessions of a limited nature for the sake of expediency. And with the insidious cunning which is one of their most effective tools in every enterprise, they have succeeded in fomenting distrust by various Christian denominations of each other, and in promoting a jealous and suspicious division between and even within denominations, which everywhere lessens the strength of opposition to Communism on the part of any Christian group. John Birch was, and clearly would have remained, a

93

militant enemy of their strategy and an unreachable exposer of their tactics, in all of these designs. His Christianity was not on the defensive, dissipating its strength in disproving calculated libels. He was a leader of a Christian offensive to carry a sense of Christian brotherhood and tolerance and justice to all the world. And at an early age he had already matured too much for the Communists to have been able to muddy his understanding, or to deflect him from his purpose, by any amount of their sophomoric mental poisons.

A second cardinal belief of Christianity, bitterly condemned by the Communists, is in the worth and importance of each individual human being. This belief John Birch exemplified in every word and deed. To the Communists fifteen million men suffering unending misery in slave labor camps are just so many pawns being used in a game, and not worth a second thought in connection with the winning of that game. To John Birch, driving the Japs from China was a lofty and overpowering cause, to which many lesser causes might properly be sacrificed. But not one single missionary was he willing to leave to die of starvation or mistreatment, even though the evacuation of some one missionary might cost heavily in plane time and fuel and human effort that otherwise would be devoted directly to winning the war. And not one Chinese child, Christian or non-Christian, was he willing to see suffer, when any practicable effort or sacrifice on his part could prevent it.

In some of the subtle Communist propaganda that has permeated every American medium of communication over the past many years, the suggestion has been carefully planted, for the gullible to dig out and proudly flaunt as their penetrating discovery, that the poor abused persecuted Communists are today's version of the early Christian martyrs. There are many things wrong with this insinuating and deceptive thesis, but one fallacy vitiates the whole body of the claim. That is, the true Christian martyr of the early centuries was willing himself to die for his belief, but he didn't want anybody else to die for it, not even his enemies. He was especially willing to die for it rather than lie about it. Your Communist, on the other hand, is very anxious that others—including, but by no means limited to, his enemies—shall die for his cause by the millions. But the Communists use every known means of blaming their actions on others, as in the case of the Katyn Massacre; of getting others to fight their battles for them, as in the seduction of idealistic American innocents into the "Abraham Lincoln Brigade"; and of personally escaping, rather than suffering for, the consequences of their own crimes against society when caught. Sometimes they even have to drive their own soldiers, with guns at their backs more threatening than those in front, as at Stalingrad. As for individual Communists standing firm for their faith under stress, they are willing to do so at the cost of ranting in public, or of reviling or torturing other people; but lying about it, to escape the consequences of their worship of Communism, is a fundamental "virtue" of their cult.

We are told that in the twenties in Europe, and in the thirties in Asia, there were some Communists who preferred and accepted death rather than deny their faith. Certainly there have been Communists who would have been willing to do so. For retrogressive, cruel, stupid, and full of childishly incongruous monstrosities as this communist philosophy may be, it has caught with its deceptive mirages the mesmerized gaze and devotion of many noble men and sincere idealists. But the custom of martyrdom has been discouraged, and the martyrs forgotten, by the Communists themselves. And the reason for the complete difference between early Christianity and today's Communism in this respect lies in the principle we are discussing, that to the Communist the individual is of too little importance for any such deliberate self-sacrifice of the individual's life to make sense. Even when some few individuals, such as the Rosenbergs, have been executed according to the compulsions of the social organization which they were seeking to destroy, the Communists have made it clear that their interest in these executions, even for propaganda value, was as a means of more rapidly publicizing their own lies and distortions of fact. They seize such opportunities to break down confidence in the civilized procedures by which even a humane society tries to protect itself against those who would undermine it through criminal betrayal. They have no sentimental concern with the individuals executed.

To the Communist the individual is always expendable, for even the slightest contribution to the cause—or for the elimination of the slightest obstruction to the cause. To a Christian, even the lowliest individual is never expendable, either positively as a sacrifice to the cause of Christian civilization, or negatively for the vilest form of blasphemy against Christianity itself, without all the protection that the circumstances of war or peace will possibly permit, and even then with only the gravest anxiety and misgivings. According to official records, John Birch "stuck his neck out" more than any other man in China, during the whole three years he was engaged in the war there, to live up to this principle of Christian humanity. It was another principle, in the necessary dilution of which, and in the ultimate banishment of which from the minds and actions of men, the Communists found and would have continued to find John Birch their implacable enemy.

A third tenet of Christianity, which the Communists cannot allow to survive, is that there can be coexistence of temporal power and organized spiritual power in the same state at the same time. Christians have accepted this as theory from the earliest days. They have observed it, with varying degrees of encroachment, throughout the centuries. The Communists have denied it, both in theory and in practice, from the very beginning of the Communist conspiracy.

The Christian, provided his freedom of worship, and of support of his church, is not denied or interfered with, is perfectly willing to pay the taxes, observe the laws, and support the sovereignty in temporal matters, of a duly constituted completely secular government. He does not see this as a divided allegiance, but as two separate non-conflicting allegiances. The Communists, being unwilling to allow any allegiance— to the family, to friends, to organizations, or to causes—other than allegiance to the Communist state, for fear that there might be conflict between this allegiance and some other, cannot even consider allowing organized religion to exert or possess any material strength or even unified spiritual influence. If the Christian thought like a Communist, he would have to destroy the *state*. Since a Communist thinks as he does, he must destroy not only religion, but the *church*. Since the Christian does not think this way, he can work for his church and patriotically support the state at the same time. And the Communists thus find this principle of social organization a reinforced bulwark against their making subservient satellites out of Christian nations.

John Birch understood this principle very well. He had been raised in a country where its soundness was taken completely for granted. Nothing in his more mature experience caused him to doubt its soundness in the least. His most evangelistic crusading on behalf of Christianity in the most pagan corners of Asia would not have given the temporal rulers of those corners the slightest reason to distrust his efforts from a civil point of view—unless they were Communists—or to put any obstacles in the way of his conversion of the natives to Christianity. But every such conversion would have meant one more cell of stronger resistance to the Communists when they came. How bitterly they hate Asiatic Christians, and the influence of the Christianity of John Birch and other missionaries among the Asiatics, is revealed by the recent report from inside Red China. They are temporarily permitting the resumption, under certain carefully humiliating restrictions, of Christian worship in some of the strongest Christian centers. Those who are ardent enough in their faith are innocently rushing like schools of fish to seize the tempting bait. And the Communist tyrants are already gloating that they will thus know who are the irreconcilables and stalwarts left among the population, to be liquidated in the next general purge. It is a cruel formula which the Communists have used many times before.

Last and most important of the philosophical and spiritual conflicts between Christianity and Communism, which we shall discuss here, is the Communist belief that the end justi-

97

fies the means and the Christian conviction that this is one of Satan's most tempting lies. For this is, by ultimate analysis, the one firm foundation of our quarrel with the Communists and with the socialists who support them with this same rationalization. And the argument is tied to John Birch not only through his holding a belief contrary to the Communist doctrine, but by his being a victim of that doctrine in its actual implementation.

None of us knows beyond all question that a socialist or communist organization of society, such as the Communists claim to desire, would not make for a happier world. We do not believe it, and there are sound reasons in historical experience, in philosophic reasoning, and in intuitive integration of the infinite guides to the pursuit of happiness, which support our contrary conviction and encourage our resistance. But we are willing to deny ourselves that claim to infallibility which we condemn so in the Communists. We are willing to grant that, conceivably, they could be right.

If the Communists and their socialist allies would depend, therefore, on persuasion rather than coercion, on an honest presentation of their arguments and blueprints rather than on opportunistic crimes of every nature, to advance their cause, we should have no right nor reason to condemn them. The men, for instance, who founded the Intercollegiate Socialist Society to which we referred above, were not criminals or scoundrels. On the contrary they were, almost without exception, idealistic young men motivated by the noblest aims. It was only as some of them, swept along by the encouragement of their fellows into a growing fanaticism about their own superior wisdom, joined the Communist criminal conspiracy or at least began to condone the use of any means to bring about a socialist society, that they lost the right to our admiration no matter how completely we disagreed with them. But over the years many of these "liberal" idealists, even those who claim that they hate Communism, acquired a blind spot, like that caused an automobile driver by the windshield support at either end, for the dirty tactics, all the way up to murder, of the Communists themselves, whenever they thought the Communists were advancing the cause of socialism. For condoning such tactics they deserve our contempt. For running interference for such tactics they deserve careful investigation. For actually participating in such tactics they deserve to be prosecuted, with energy and justice, according to our civilized laws. For even good ends do not justify foul means. And a whole civilization—the best our poor fumbling, bungling race has yet arrived at—has been painfully built on the principle that the individual or the mob must be limited by law in the means chosen to achieve its ends. Neither the Communists, their fellow travelers, nor their philosophically kindred socialists, have any such prima facie case that they are right and we are wrong as to justify their reversion to barbarism to establish their desired form of social organization.

Your true Christian, like John Birch, will not even stand passively on the sidelines and allow crimes against the code of a Christian civilization to be perpetrated without protest and militant action. He had already sensed the beginning of sinister events in China before he died. During the last months of the war he wrote home that the American diplomats and leaders in China had much to answer for, and that when he returned to America he would have some surprising things to tell.

As Captain Birch, he willingly cooperated with the Chinese Communists during the war whenever the occasion arose. And there is no doubt that, so long as his natural American ignorance of the nature and extent of the Communist conspiracy remained, and if the Communists appeared to exert their control according to civilized standards, he would have felt that the coexistence of a Nationalist Government and a Communist Government in China was not his concern. But as soon as the Communists began to reveal their true nature; to wreck every effort of the Nationalist Government to reestablish communications, industry, and the whole economy on a peaceful basis; to turn loose their flood of lies about Chiang Kai-shek, in America, and about Americans, in China; to murder, and pillage, and destroy, John Birch would not even have had to stop to commune with himself as to whether their philosophy and professed aims were good or bad. He would have used all the force of his convincing voice and determined energy, supported by a thorough personal knowledge of the Chinese scene, to deny their lies and to try to stop their destructiveness. When all the rest of humanity, except the Communists, were looking forward to peace and rehabilitation, ten days after the Japanese surrender, the very group that murdered John Birch, at that very time, were engaged in tearing up railroad tracks and tearing down telephone wires, for the specific purpose of causing misery and despair to the civilian population. And they were quite right in assuming that, whatever their ends, their means alone would have made John Birch a foe who could not be silenced except by death.

By one of those dramatic coincidences which the tempo of war makes common, it so happens that John Birch expressed himself on some of the Christian principles we have been discussing, in the last letter which he ever wrote. It was begun on August 13, 1945 (August 12 in America), to his parents in Georgia. Added to and continued off and on, according to habit, and obviously brought to a close on August 15 with forgivable abruptness, it did not reach Mr. and Mrs. Birch until after the news of their son's death. And it seems worth while, as a fitting end to this chapter, to incorporate that short letter here in full. To paraphrase one paragraph in it, John Birch wanted peace, for all people and for many reasons, with all his heart. But he would never have been willing to accept peace, even for a short time, when purchased by a tolerance of such evils as he would soon have seen the Communists spreading across China and the world.

China, August 13, 1945

Dear Folks:

Here at my little outpost we are all waiting for President Truman's word tonight concerning Japan's answer to the Allied qualification of the first surrender offer. Yesterday, Sunday morning, I held a service especially thanking God for bringing us to the eve of victory, and all my men voluntarily attended except one operator who had to stay by the transmitter. We have been holding Sunday morning services every week that I am here to lead them. This has been the case for several months now.

The C.I.M. have a splendid group of Christians at Fowyang, Anhwei; I preached to six hundred plus of them there on Sunday morning not long ago, at the invitation of the pastor. It was the first time I have preached in Chinese since leaving Changsha.

Father, do not worry about my "turning back in the furrow." I may "make tents" in my own way; but as long as it pleases God to use my voice for preaching His Gospel, I expect to be doing that.

Please convey the following message to George Stanley, wherever he may be. Dear George S.: Congratulations on your marriage to as fine a person as I'm sure Alice is. I think often of you both, despite the evidence of my poor letter writing to the contrary. I do want to take issue with a statement you made—but surely cannot have meant—in a letter forwarded to me by Betty. You said: "At best this or any other war is just 'beating our heads against the wall' . . . all fighting and winning is temporary only." I will admit that much of what we rightly "render to Caesar" is of a temporary nature, because it is all in the present life. But many of these temporary things are of high importance and enjoined by God (as the execution of wrath upon evildoers by human governments). To me, it is of the utmost importance to gain the temporary opportunity to preach Christ's Gospel! Have you ever seen a humble Chinese brother, who was beheaded because he preached Christ rather than the Emperor of Japan? I have. To me it is of high importance that peace-loving Chinese peasants be allowed to live out their lives in peace!

Have you ever watched a Jap soldier steal the pitifully few grains of rice belonging to a large family of starving children? I have. Have you ever seen Chinese girls after the Japanese machine-gunned them? I have.

I want peace, but not that purchased by tolerance of such evils as I saw Japan spreading across this part of the world!

Without much military training or knowledge, excepting brief observation of fights between Japs and guerillas in Chekiang,

I tried to volunteer as a private, but they made me a second lieutenant instead. Since that day I have tried, as wholeheartedly as I could, to serve the flag that had protected my life so far. If you had ever lived for one day under the shadow of the Jap secret police, you would thank God that America had enough "suckers," as you call them, to redden the sands of Tarawa or drop flaming to death through the China skies; that there were enough "suckers" to stop the Imperial Navy at Midway and the Jab bombers at Kunming.

Word has just come over the radio that Japan has unconditionally surrendered. Praise God from Whom all blessings flow! No, brother of mine, we did not vainly beat our hands against a wall; we cut our hands smashing the teeth of a monstrous mouth that was devouring, and that rapidly, the lives, land, liberty, and happiness of poor helpless human beings in many parts of the world. And now that mouth, even though it be temporarily, is *closed!* Yes, George, liberty is worth its price!

Good night, and love to all.

John

XIX

The War Is Now

IT IS THE purpose of this small book to ensure that John Birch did not die in vain. It is true that, at the time, we were deliberately denied the opportunity to know or to evaluate the circumstances, the forces, or the philosophy which his murder might have made more clear. As a consequence his sacrifice contributed nothing to our needed enlightenment, during the past nine years while the octopus of Communism was reaching its creepy tentacles ever more penetratingly over the whole planet. But even now his story may still serve to throw one more needed beam of light on the nature and the aims, the strategy and the tactics, of the conspiracy that will destroy us unless we expose and destroy it first. If so, one thing of which we can be gratefully certain is that John Birch would have considered his own life and death to have been very much worth while. •

For it seems to me, and to many like me, that we now face, directly and with ominous nearness, the most transcendent crisis within not only the recorded and semi-recorded history of the human race, but within the biological history of the human species. We have already mentioned, among probabilities now threatening us, the enslavement of America and all other free nations, the destruction of a whole civilization that has been thousands of years in the building, and the ruthless substitution of the temporal religion of communism for all spiritual religions—the last danger including the extermination from the human tradition of those principles of morals, ethics, and humanity which have been common denominators of the great religions. To any human being who is not mentally blind, even to those who are proponents of communism for whatever cause, these are clear and present dangers.

But there are two more dangers, which reach beyond even these threats in their ultimate consequences. One is obvious. Through mishandling of celestial powers by little men, either for conquest or for defense, the explosive or radioactive forces of hydrogen or cobalt atoms in chain reaction may get out of hand and literally destroy the planet—or *all life on it*. Whether a similar catastrophe has happened once or billions of times before we have no way of knowing. The Persian poet wrote:

> And fear not lest Existence closing your
> Account, and mine, should know the like no more;
> The Eternal Sákí from that Bowl has poured
> Millions of Bubbles like us, and will pour.

It may well be—it is beyond our present knowledge to guess either way—that an Eternal Power has not only shaped millions of solar systems like our own, but has permitted the evolution of life on millions of planets within those systems. The surmise, however, is poor consolation to the heirs of a billion years of one such evolutionary climb, on the prospect of seeing themselves and their inheritance swept into nothingness.

The second possible catastrophe, of completely final import to the human race, is less obvious and slower in its operation, but no less conclusive in the long run. It derives from the fact that the communists and other socialists, instead of being infallibly right in their belief as to what is best for the human race, may be—could be—completely, irreparably, and *fatally* wrong. The possibility is sufficiently ominous to justify deeply thoughtful attention for two or three painful paragraphs.

For civilization is evidently just one, of an infinite number, of the evolutionary contrivances of nature. It might be seized upon, by any dominant species of a necessary minimum intelligence, at a certain advanced stage in its struggle for survival and growth. And it is apt eventually to be over-used, to the dangerous detriment of the species, like any other physical or psychical adaptation to circumstances.

And civilization, or the progress of the species by means of and during civilization, depends on competition with members of other species being entirely supplanted by competition between individuals within the species. This competition, being between equals who were alike in physical endowments, has, in our own case, had far greater impact on man's mental growth than on his physical adaptation. The result has produced not only you and me, in our proud superiority to the other primates, but the opportunity for the development of a human being as far superior to ourselves, in mental stature, as we are to the apes.

But collectivism, then, is more than the tragic *sociological* mistake for civilized man which we have already discussed. Collectivism is a *biological* false path; not only a retrogressive tendency in any species which has reached any of the higher evolutionary stages, but one of Nature's perenially unsuccessful experimental tangents which always ultimately ends

104

in a "blind alley." This fatal *cul de sac* quality of collectivism—
and of its even darker tributary tangents, such as Communism
and mass slavery—stands starkly revealed by a hundred million years of insect history.

If, therefore, the Communists or any of their philosophical
descendants succeed in fastening the regimented non-competitive organization of life and of effort onto *all human beings, everywhere on the planet,* the growth of *homo sapiens*
will have ended. If this ant-like system of non-competitive cooperation is established with sufficient rapidity and universal-
ity for only the few generations needed, to have it automatically (and after a while instinctively) accepted, as the natural
pattern of human activity; and if there are no exceptions left
anywhere on the planet to suggest otherwise; then the increasingly rare individuals who might wish to rebel against
the system will have no more chance of flaunting the commu-
nity conscience than would a lone ant that tried to hoard and
hide some of the nest's honeydew for her own personal use.

Man, thereafter, in unhappy stagnation of intellect at its
present level, will simply exist through the ensuing millenia
until environmental changes occur, or outside competition
arises, with which our species cannot cope. If the planet itself
lasts long enough man will then disappear in time, as surely
as will the ant, as surely as did the dinosaur, and for the same
basic reason. This possible catastrophe is not fanciful, and is
not one which man, at his present fortunate stage of understanding of himself and his universe, should be stupid enough
to ignore.

But this has been, necessarily, too slight an excursion into
too deep a subject. This particular danger was included in
our list only for the sake of an honest completeness; and we
have no quarrel with any reader who wishes to discount it.
The other dangers are too palpable, and too imminent.

For the Communists are rapidly proceeding right now,
with visible daily progress on almost every front, towards the
successful achievement of their total goals. And they are doing so, in the remaining free and semi-free nations of the

globe, by use of exactly the same means that they have used for the capture of every sizable country, including Russia itself, since they first gained a foothold from which to operate. These means consist primarily of infiltration, deception, indoctrination, and the gradual seizure of power, *from within.* When any man tells you today that the danger of Communism, to America, is not from within our country, but from without, that we should stop worrying about the Communists and their sympathizers in our midst and worry only about their armies and their possessions outside, he is either a pro-Communist, completely uninformed, or naive beyond reason. For he is denying all experience, a huge total of very tragic experience indeed, with this unappeasable enemy. And what is true of America is true of every major country still outside of the Iron Curtain.

Except in very weak adjacent states like Latvia and Finland, and in areas which were pre-conquered for them by Hitler or the Allies, like Poland and East Germany, the Russian Communists have not anywhere risked the direct use of their own armed forces. They have, when infiltration and treason have made the time ripe, maneuvered Spaniards (with volunteers from other nations) into fighting Spaniards, Yugoslavs into fighting Yugoslavs, Chinese into fighting Chinese, or North Koreans into fighting South Koreans. They have sent equipment and technicians and strategists into these frays, to help those fighting on the Communist side. But their technique has been to take over every country, when their infiltration and treason had gone far enough, by a peaceful coup if possible, or by bloody *internal civil* war if necessary; never by conquering arms from without. Guatemala[2] has recently fallen to Communist control; Italy may fall at any time. But the Communists have never had *one regiment* of "foreign" soldiers in either Guatemala or Italy, nor even threatening their borders. They have now used this technique, continuously and successfully, in country after country, large and small, for decades. Except as noted above, they have never used any other. With it, in just the last ten years, they have added six hundred million people to their slave empire; and have reached the point that their threat is serious and immediate in half of the world that still remains unconquered. They are so obviously using the same technique in America, so confidently, patiently, and justifiably counting on its ultimate success, that only the willfully blind can honestly deny the growing menace any longer.

The truth is terrifying but inescapable. The pressure exerted on American public opinion, and directly within our government, by the Communists and their dupes and allies, is so subtle and insidious, so clever and well-planned, so invisible and unrecognized, and still so extensive and cumulatively overwhelming, that it sweeps even our ablest and most patriotic diplomats and administrators down its patiently chosen path. The world-wide Communist hierarchy thrives on prestige and the aura of success, far more than on what it wins by bullets or by bombs. And yet we go on handing them one diplomatic victory, one prestige-building success, after another, practically on a silver platter. And the overall results prove conclusively, however much the infinite details and separate events may be argued about, that treason is the strongest force pulling the strings that guide us. For as James Forrestal so truthfully complained, if it were only stupidity that dictated our course in foreign affairs, some of the mistakes would be on our side.

There are probably not more than twenty-five thousand traitors in this country, today, in a population of one hundred and sixty million. But every single one of those twenty-five thousand is a fanatic. Almost every one has a warped but functionally brilliant mind, because it is to that kind of mentality that Communism most strongly appeals. Every one of the twenty-five thousand is committed, in his whole being and purpose, to the conquest of America by Communist doctrine and the eventual rule of America by Communist masters. This goal is not something additional to his private ambition, to be given the leavings of his energy. It is, to him, the reason for his existence, to which all other aims and efforts

107

are contributory or merely incidental. He is determined to do his full part towards bringing about this Communist victory by any means, for the end is all that matters. He accepts the discipline of those who plan Communist strategy, fully aware that the reins of that discipline and that planning lead all the way back to Moscow. To further Communist strategy, even when he does not understand it, he will strive for positions of honor, and do his best to promote other Communists into similar positions. He will concoct policies that are two-edged, knowing that the edge which damages American interests is the one that will be pressed effectively. Disguised as a patriot, he will distort the aims of true patriots, and help to ruin their careers, while building up the prestige of other traitors like himself. He will lie and steal and even murder, if necessary, though he usually prefers to have the murder done remotely, if possible, through the effect of his policies, rather than by his own hands. If so ordered he will, by patient guile over the years, make of himself a respected leader in labor or law or education or any field, without the slightest visible trace of any Communist connection, in order that he may work behind the scenes for Communist aims. Posing as a humanitarian liberal, he will multiply the reach of his own voice a hundred or a thousand fold by beguiling honest liberals to follow his bellowing like so many sheep. For the "egghead" that talks like a Communist is of small importance compared to the real Communist who pretends to be an egghead.

It was these traitors and their dupes and allies who kept the story of John Birch from the American people, most of them without ever having heard of John Birch themselves. It would be easier for us to write the final chapter of this book in a more restrained tone, and to hew more closely to the line of orthodox biography. But this would be a betrayal of the aims for which John Birch gave his life. For the tremendous cumulative direct power and indirect influence of these same traitors, their further converts, their dupes and allies is still with us and still far-reaching.

And we are at a crossroads where their influence may be decisive; a crossroads not just of a nation, nor even just of a civilization, but of the human race itself. It is the first time since man began to spread over the planet that the fate of the whole race has been at stake in any struggle. One road leads easily and appealingly down, eventually to slavery, stagnation, and increasing darkness. The other leads up the winding and difficult road to greater freedom, further growth and more enlightenment. And as if it were not enough temptation to the spirit of man to see the apparently easier road before him, there are charmers who would seduce and slave-masters who would drive him to make the leftward, downward turn.

We have built this sermon around John Birch, for in one blade of grass lies the key to all creation, could we only understand it; and in the forces that swirled around John Birch lay all the conflicts, of philosophy and of implementation, with which our whole world is now so imperatively concerned. *Therein lay the significance of his life and death.* Actually we must choose between the civilization, the form of society, and the expression of human life, as represented by John Birch, and their parallels as envisioned by Karl Marx and his spiritual successors. There is no middle ground, at least for the foreseeable future; not because no middle ground is philosophically possible, nor because intelligent and humane beings could not prefer some middle ground, but because the Communists will not permit it. The man who stands ideologically half way between John Birch and a young Malenkov or Vishinsky has no more chance of ultimate survival in a state once thoroughly subdued by the Communists than did Captain Birch himself. The Communists will use compromise, to serve their purpose; but will not permit compromise to stand, once that purpose has been carried out. Not only are you either with the Communists or against them. By their own determined and ruthless delineation, you are either with them *all the way*, without a shadow of a reservation, or you are one hundred per cent their enemy after you have served their purpose. This is a principle which those who would compromise with Communism, or with Communists, should learn well and never forget. It is far more literally true, in dealing with Communism, than it was in dealing with the evil Lowell had in mind, that "they enslave their children's children who make compromise with sin."

John Birch was just an American farm boy who might have been your son or mine. But he was the first, or very nearly the first, casualty in American uniform, in a war still being waged against us nine years later; a relentless war of which there is no end in sight. John Birch was killed by typical Communist tactics, as a part of typical Communist strategy, in a typical Communist-style war—a continuous undeclared war which observes no rules of international law, of civilization, or of human decency. He commanded no armies, headed no government, converted no nations to his creed. His impact would have been of transient memory and comparatively small importance, had not that impact occurred at a time and in a way to make it supply particulars from which momentous generalizations can properly be projected. *With his death and in his death the battle lines were drawn, in a struggle from which either Communism or Christian-style civilization must emerge with one completely triumphant and the other completely destroyed.*

As John lay dying during that last hour or two of agony, after he had been shot and bayonetted and his body tossed aside, he must have realized that the rise of anti-Christ, which he had foreseen, was already upon us. There is no way in which we can reach back, across the nine-year interval, and let him know that his death was not in vain. But what really matters, what would have mattered most to John Birch, is whether his sacrifice does in fact help to awaken his countrymen to their danger and their duty; and whether his career does help to inspire them to revere more sincerely, and to protect more devotedly, that hard-earned freedom, as a birthright of all men, for which he fought so well. If we rediscover some of our sounder spiritual values in the example of his life, recharge our determination from the spark of his courage, and learn essential truths about our enemy from the lesson of his murder, then his death at twenty-six ceases to be a tragedy. For in a full lifetime he could not have accomplished more.

NOTES

1. Further details concerning this memorandum may be found on Pages 218 and 219 of William Henry Chamberlin's *America's Second Crusade.*

2. Since these lines were written a successful uprising has taken Guatemala—temporarily, at least, and we hope permanently—out of the list of Communist-controlled countries. But this does not alter the fact that the Communists had reached so far; that they had established an actual Communist government among our near neighbors in Central America; that they had done so entirely by infiltration from within; and that further and more lastingly successful results of such infiltration, in both Central and South America, are inevitable unless we begin to show a great deal more firmness and dependable leadership in our opposition to the Communists.

READING LIST

READING LIST

THIS narrative account of the life of John Birch is put together almost entirely from previously unpublished sources. The outline of events and developments which portray the times in which John Birch lived and died, on the other hand, is drawn entirely from the published work of historians, journalists, and essayists, many of whom have had to blaze their own trails of truth through a wilderness of deliberate obfuscation. Here, as in the case of my earlier small book, *May God Forgive Us,* I have simply been assembling and arranging second-hand materials, in an effort to give more continuity and clarity to the story which they tell.

My debts, therefore, to others who have done the conscientious research work and factual reporting, or who have by their own efforts exposed pieces of the Communist conspiracy, are too numerous and heavy to be cleared up by any perfunctory acknowledgment such as this. I can only hope that these pioneers will forgive my brazen borrowing, for the sake of the greater effectiveness given their disclosures by every repetition. This is particularly true with regard to James Burnham's *The Web Of Subversion,* Shafer and Snow's *The Turning Of The Tides,* and George Racey Jordan's *From Major Jordan's Diaries.* It is true to only a slightly lesser extent of at least a dozen other books in the list below, and to some extent of almost all of them.

Because I am neither a scholar, historian, reporter, nor commentator, but primarily a business man, I am well aware of the difficulty the ordinary citizen has in identifying and finding the periodicals and books which will give him the plain and undoctored truth about various parts of our recent history. For the Communists, their dupes, and allies have been far more successful in smothering such publications by their insidious and unceasing pressures than most Americans will believe. I am, therefore, adding here a partial list of both books and periodicals which reveal the Communist activities and successes, of the past and the present. To anybody who wants to know the frightening facts of the world-wide war we are steadily losing, I particularly recommend the volumes that are starred.

Periodicals

The American Mercury, 11 East 36th Street, New York 16, New York

The Freeman, Irvington Press, Irvington-on-Hudson, N. Y.

Human Events, 1835 K Street, N.W., Washington, D.C.

Marjorie Shearon's *Challenge to Socialism*, Shearon Legislative Service, 9127 Jones Mill Road, Chevy Chase 15, Maryland

Faith and Freedom, Spiritual Mobilization, 1521 Wilshire Boulevard, Los Angeles 17, California

Headlines, 342 Madison Avenue, New York 17, New York

Economic Council Letter, National Economic Council, Inc., Empire State Building, New York 1, New York

The New Leader, 7 East 15th Street, New York 3, New York

Counterattack, 55 West 42nd Street, New York 36, New York

Intelligence Digest, 14 Old Queen Street, Westminster, London, S.W.1, England

American Legion Magazine, Circulation Department, P.O. Box 1055, Indianapolis 6, Indiana

U. S. News & World Report, Circulation Department, 437 Parker Avenue, Dayton 1, Ohio

Older Books

Abend, Hallet: *Half Slave, Half Free* (Bobbs)

Barmine, Alexander: *One Who Survived* (Putnam)

Barnes, Harry Elmer: *The Struggle Against The Historical Blackout* (National Council for American Education, New York)

Belgion, Montgomery: *Victor's Justice* (Regnery)

*Bentley, Elizabeth: *Out of Bondage* (Devin-Adair)

Borkenau, Franz: *European Communism* (Harper)
Budenz, Louis: *The Cry Is Peace* (Regnery)
Budenz, Louis: *Men Without Faces* (Harper)
Calomiris, Angela: *Red Masquerade* (Lippincott)
Caldwell and Frost: *The Korea Story* (Regnery)
**Chamberlin, William H.: *America's Second Crusade* (Regnery)
*Chambers, Whittaker: *Witness* (Random House)
Ciechanowski, Jan: *Defeat In Victory* (Doubleday)
*Creel, George: *Russia's Race For Asia* (Bobbs)
Dallin, David: *The Rise Of Russia In Asia* (Yale Univ. Press)
Dallin, David: *Russia And Postwar Europe* (Yale Univ. Press)
Dallin, David: *Soviet Russia and the Far East* (Yale Univ. Press)
Dallin, David: *Soviet Russia's Foreign Policy,* 1939-1942 (Yale Univ. Press)
Dallin, David; and B. I. Nicolaevsky: *Forced Labor in Soviet Russia* (Yale Univ. Press)
Deane, John R.: *The Strange Alliance* (Viking)
de Toledano, Ralph: *Spies, Dupes, and Diplomats* (Duell, Sloane & Pierce)
*Dies, Martin: *The Trojan Horse In America* (Dodd, Mead & Company)
Ebon, Martin: *World Communism Today* (Whittlesey)
Fitch, Geraldine: *Formosa Beachhead* (Regnery)
*Flynn, John T.: *While You Slept* (Devin-Adair)
Gitlow, Benjamin: *The Whole Of Their Lives* (Scribner)
*Jordan, George R.: *From Major Jordan's Diaries* (Harcourt, Brace & Company)
Kravchenko, Victor: *I Chose Freedom* (Scribner)
*Lane, Arthur Bliss: *I Saw Poland Betrayed*
**Lasky, Victor and Ralph de Toledano: *Seeds of Treason* (Funk)
Lin Yutang: *The Vigil of a Nation* (Day)
Lipper, Elinor: *Eleven Years In Soviet Prison Camps* (Regnery)
*Lyons, Eugene: *The Red Decade* (Bobbs)
*Martin, David: *Ally Betrayed* (Prentice-Hall)
Maurer, Herrymon: *Collision of East and West* (Regnery)
Mikolajczyk, Stanislaw: *The Rape of Poland* (Whittlesey)
Moorad, George: *Behind the Iron Curtain* (Fireside Press)
Philbrick, Herbert: *I Led Three Lives* (McGraw-Hill)
Reinhardt, Guenther: *Crime Without Punishment* (Hermitage)
*Roe, Wellington: *Juggernaut* (Lippincott)

Salanzar, Sanchez: *Murder In Mexico* (Secker and Warburg)
Sanborn, Frederic R.: *Design For War* (Devin-Adair)
Serge, Victor: *Russia Twenty Years After* (Pioneer Publishers)
Smith, Andrew: *I Was A Soviet Worker* (Robert Hale)
Souvarine, Boris: *Stalin* (Alliance)
Spolansky, Jacob: *The Communist Trail in America* (MacMillan)
*Stripling, Robert: *The Red Plot Against America* (Bell)
Tansill, Charles Callan: *Back Door To War* (Regnery)
Tokaev, G. A.: *Stalin Means War* (George Weidenfeld & Nicholson, Ltd., London)
Utley, Freda: *The China Story* (Regnery)
Utley, Freda: *Last Chance in China* (Bobbs)
Utley, Freda: *The High Cost of Vengeance* (Regnery)
Veale, F.J.P.: *Advance to Barbarism* (C. C. Nelson)
*White, Leigh: *Balkan Caesar* (Scribners)
Willoughby, Charles A.: *Shanghai Conspiracy* (Dutton)

More Current Books

Anisimov, Oleg: *The Ultimate Weapon* (Regnery)
*Burnham, James: *The Web of Subversion* (John Day)
Buckley and Bozell: *McCarthy And His Enemies* (Regnery)
Budenz, Louis: *The Techniques of Communism* (Regnery)
Dallin, David: *The New Soviet Empire* (Yale Univ. Press)
Fellers, Bonner: *Wings For Peace* (Regnery)
Flynn, John T.: *The Lattimore Story* (Devin-Adair)
Grenfell, Russell: *Unconditional Hatred* (Devin-Adair)
King-Hall, Stephen: *The Communist Conspiracy* (MacMillan)
*Manly, Chesly: *The Twenty Year Revolution* (Regnery)
Muhlen, Norbert: *The Return of Germany* (Regnery)
Shafer and Snow: *The Turning of the Tides* (Long House)
Theobald, Robert A.: *The Final Secret of Pearl Harbor* (Devin-Adair)
Wilbur, William H.: *Guideposts to the Future* (Regnery)
Wittmer, Felix: *The Yalta Betrayal* (Caxton)
Wormser, Rene: *The Myth of the Good and Bad Nations* (Regnery)

CPSIA information can be obtained
at www.ICGtesting.com
Printed in the USA
BVHW040301060821
613445BV00010B/988

9 781163 817476